The Best American Short Plays

2003-2004

The Best American Short Plays

2003-2004

edited with an introduction
by Glenn Young

APPLAUSE
THEATRE & CINEMA BOOKS

The Best American Short Plays 2003-2004
edited by Glenn Young

Copyright © 2006 by Applause Theatre & Cinema Books

All rights reserved

Book design by Pearl Chang

ISBN-13: 978-1-55783-695-3 ISBN-10:1-55783-695-7 [cloth]
ISBN-13: 978-1-55783-696-0 ISBN-10:1-55783-696-5 [paper]
ISSN: 0067-6284

Applause Theatre & Cinema Books
19 West 21st Street, Suite 201
New York, NY 10010
Phone: (212) 575-9265
Fax: (212) 575-9270
Email: info@applausepub.com
Internet: www.applausepub.com

Applause books are available through your local bookstore, or you may order at www.applausepub.com or call Music Dispatch at 800-637-2852

Sales & Distribution

North America:
Hal Leonard Corp.
7777 West Bluemound Road
P. O. Box 13819
Milwaukee, WI 53213
Phone: (414) 774-3630
Fax: (414) 774-3259
Internet: www.halleonard.com
Email: halinfo@halleonard.com

Europe:
Roundhouse Publishing Ltd.
Millstone, Limers Lane
Northam, North Devon EX 39 2RG
Phone: (0) 1237-474-474
Fax: (0) 1237-474-774
Email: roundhouse.group@ukgateway.net

contents

introduction
by Glenn Young

Post–A–Bomb, when every act was potentially one's last, second acts seemed irrelevant. A second act presupposed one string of actions predictably leading to another. But Predictability was the last thing the world could claim after the Atom Bomb. Overnight, "cause and effect" became quaint terms of an obsolete world order. The structure of expectations throughout the physical, moral, and psychological worlds shattered into bits of old fine china. Indeed, Mr. Heisenberg had already proved this to be a universal truth in his famous Uncertainty Principle. In a nanosecond of U.S. hubris over Hiroshima, the Future became a thing of the past. Noël Coward, whose devil-may-care humor had bolstered sagging spirits through the war, became an outcast in post-WWII London, his dramatic etiquette an affront to current reality. Nothing, certainly no full-length play, was so well made that it could withstand the force of the New Apocalypse. This Armageddon was not scripted in Revelations but unleashed in a garbled postscript to a war whose victory was a foregone conclusion by men with unprecedented destructive power. The Bomb created a new concatenation of non sequitur that would rewire the dramaturgical consciousness through its new electricians: Beckett, Ionesco, Pinter, and Genet. The one-act play had become the natural heir to the stage.

And then it happened all over again. The pinprick of time that September morning in 2001 exploded Americans' way of keeping time in much the same way half a century earlier, America's bombing of Hiroshima had ripped through the world's Cartesian complacencies. Just when people were thinking it was safe to go back into the Futures market again, when long dramatic arcs again seemed to repli-cate life, the Uncertainty Principle struck back. On 9/11, the American Dream of hard work and an endless upside turned horrific when, in a split second, the cumu-lative industry of nearly 3,000 mostly highly successful Americans went up in vapor and settled down ominously across the city, and the civilized world, as ash. From dust thou art. How can you afford to have an intermission in a Manhattan theatre when the entire audience is thinking only of the nearest emergency exit?

No dramatic structure may be better suited to clarify the particulate haze that beclouds the American consciousness post-9/11 than the one-act play's high com-pression and explosive entrances and exits. It has the power to distract us from the abyss even as it throws it in our face. The short play is a natural habitat for free rad-icals, escaped tangents, and stray soliloquies. Even Heisenberg might have been certain of that.

Jules Tasca

In **THE DEATH OF BLISS**, Jules Tasca takes the politics of terrorism home for dinner. He renders a political apocalypse in slow motion, breaking it down into its domestic parts. Khalid's honor at being chosen as a suicide bomber is not following the romantic script drafted by his handlers. Khalid envisages a martyr's funeral with his coffin raised high and thousands chanting his name as Allah's disciple and imag-ines Sana, the sainted widow he will leave behind, revered with every wish tended to. He rapturously envisions the long embrace before she grudgingly relinquishes him to the greater good of the Muslim cause. Sana, who has already lost a brother to the cause, has lived through the romance once and found the reality wanting. She resents the obsession with Israel—regardless of how justified hatred for it may be—because it has replaced the good life they might still lead for themselves and for their people.

With Sana's news that they're going to have the child they have long prayed for, the play takes its savage ironic detour. Their future is no longer an academic exercise, a domestic difference of opinion. Must this grace of fertility be dislodged by the impersonal honor of civic sacrifice? The personal glory of Khalid's suicide is set against the resulting sacrifice of his unborn child's future. The Palestinian Authority does not concern itself with a single unborn child but with a generation of futureless unborn children. What is the nature of action? Tasca asks. Two possible second acts emerge: One, a father who sells the news at his kiosk in central Jerusalem, trades on the gossip and bonbons of polical gossip, and returns each night to raise his son or daughter. Or, the father who sees a life beyond, commits a transcendental act and survives in legend, a glorious martyr of the cause. When Khalid dons the vest that will envelop him in flames, his unborn child seems to recoil in Sana's womb.

Peter Maloney

Peter Maloney's Cassie exercises her charge at the end of a leash in Abu Ghraib prison. The playwright simultaneously flails away at our moral indignation in a subtle psychological workout. At first we feel an immediate repugnance towards Cassie's dehumanizing torture of her Iraqi prisoner. As her monologue proceeds, however, we realize that Cassie too is dehumanized by her circumstances. Her unfolding backstory shows us that Cassie didn't have all that far to travel in the humiliation business. Like the snapping turtle near her childhood home, Cassie is stuck in the swamp of her own racist upbringing. The monologue is interrupted by the orders she barks at her dog. In those pauses, the audience may be invited to intervene in the torture but, like the infamous Yale experiment, our silence confers complicity. For many in the audience, Abdul will assume the shape of the horrific photographs that first outraged world opinion.

LEASH becomes a powerful, implicit dialogue between the invisible and mute prisoner, Abdul, and the invisible silent audience. It is as if Maloney finally hands us the leash and asks us to tame its monstrous inclinations. An exercise that starts by dehumanizing the victims ends by forging an animal class out of the perpetrators. But perhaps most insidious of all, the play questions the humanity of each of us, the American citizens who unleashed Cassie in the first place.

John Guare

John Guare's protagonist immediately steps out of the choral phalanx in the Grand Jury courtroom to declare his inability to serve. His reason is unapologetic, self-centered: "It's not convenient. I'm busy. No reason." His duty to the community would spoil any plans he might make to "enjoy the spring." The John in John

Guare's **WOMAN AT A THRESHOLD BECKONING** has lived in a kind of benumbed cryogenic suspension since 9/11. His isolation is self-imposed in circumstances that brought many other New Yorkers closer together. John's a desultory impatient guy, a loner on an urgent mission to nowhere in particular. The drug indictments that the jury robotically rubber stamps have their own dulling effect, like an I.V. set up in the play's dramatic core. In the audience, one begins to feel the need for a fix—a kickstart out of the inexorable lethargy of life's paralytic routine.

Enter an Arab Woman from a world so totally beyond the jury's jingoistic moorings, it is prepared to hang her simply for the different life she represents. Our man, John, heretofore supremely unbothered by the propinquities of life, is jolted into an electric connection with this alien force. This epiphanic figure speaking through the rote diction of the official translator casts a hallucinogenic spell over John, redolent of the whirling dervishes he witnessed one birthday in Egypt. John is reborn again here in these Kafkaesque surroundings as some promise of meaning is conferred on the 9/11 devastations. John lingers in the threshold of Narima Abdullah's aura. Is ecstasy, the godlike trance outside oneself, possible in a world ceaselessly haunted by the implosions of so much precious human flesh? Human karma wasn't invented on 9/ll. It wasn't invented at Auschwitz. It was and is an immanent condition, an emulsive continuum made up as much by the memory of a warm summer evening in a precinct of Cairo where men and women convened to resemble gods.

Mary Gallagher

Mary Gallagher introduces us into a **PERFECT** world—provided one keeps score according to the Forbes Lifestyle magazine. A match conceived in Corporate Yuppie Heaven, Kitty and Dan align in their gene sequencing as perfectly as identical twins. Every genetic trait, from a Darien sense of humor to a progressive Greenwich sense of manners, matches magnificently. Dan appears to lack nothing to make him Kitty's ideal mate. No fashion makeover necessary, no sagging ab need be tweaked into perfect tone. Dandy Dan is the textbook definition of handsome young corporate potentate. And yet...and yet...—Kitty hesitates. One suspect entry in Dan's profile hangs over them like a hanging chad on a cold Florida morning. Dan's political predilections are a source of anxiety. Kitty will not fraternize with the enemy, whom she takes to be anyone from the camp of George W. Bush.

During the informal dinner set up by Binky and Tina, one can feel the political apathy gradually titrate into their souls, drip by drip, like the coffee oozing out of the new espresso machine. Her friends' passive collaboration with the status quo makes them dangerous allies in the battle of a responsible life. Tina and her thirty-something adolescent husband, Binky, and their model mate friend, Dan, will always cast their ballots as absentee citizens. They live at a corporate distance from the shareholders of American life. Kitty, even as she seems to be hurtling into bed, cannot help but be part of the Resistance.

Lavonne Mueller

As the American Army begins its bloody liberation of Normandy in Lavonne Mueller's play **THE WOUNDED DO NOT CRY**, there is an immediate reminder of the virulent anti-Semitism back on U.S. shores: "What's the Kike doing here?" challenges one officer upon sighting Frances' profile on the beach. Frances hasn't come to Europe to battle anti-Semitism. There was anti-Semitism enough to battle in America. Frances, the idealistic nurse from Boston who arrives with curlers in her hair to take on the Nazis and succor our brave warriors, has all the glamour of the Army knocked out of her as she wades ashore. The stacks of driftwood on the beach that remind her of Cape Cod turn out instead to be bodies of American young men who never made it alive out of the sea. The lost glamour is soon replaced, however, by a sturdier Yankee sensibility cauterized by experience and shot through with poetry. In Mueller's world, deep feeling becomes a dangerous luxury, an extravagance that, like poetry, may break the bank as it enriches the soul. When Lieutenant Stein is brought in for what Frances knows will prove mortal wounds, the bond is as immediate and deep as it must be brief. His last rites will be administered by a Jewish nurse from Boston who shares his love of Wilfred Owen's war verses, as both soldier and nurse expel their final aspirations together under enemy fire.

Tina Howe

The ancient pools of mythic yore reflected the temperaments of the gods and concealed their unfathomable deeds. Similarly, an Upper West Side health club whips up from its scabby sediment and detrital depths a palpable figment of an English teacher's disoriented dream. Straight from her twelfth grade class, behold! 'Tis

Ophelia, Hamlet's occasional beloved. Equally out of joint in every age, Ophelia humanizes the chlorined waters, leavens the teacher's cynical rage with exotic poesies, and reminds the lifeguard, Jesus, of the extravagant depths inside his gene pool. Tina Howe has interbred fact and fiction, time and ether, to create **WATER MUSIC**, a dramatic monstrosity that directors will aim to tame only at great risk of wading in too far over their heads.

Deborah Brevoort

Resurrected, recycled, retreaded, Elvis lives not in his multitudinous sightings around the world but in the chips of paint from Graceland, the leaves plucked from its trees by his fans, each of whom frames a private iconography of their saint. From a distance they appear as fans hysterically driven by their loss, but in Deborah Brevoort's **BLUE MOON OVER MEMPHIS**, the chorus of Elvisites (or is that Elves?) who make the annual pilgrimage to their Memphis shrine, are taken aside and, one by one, taken seriously: "I'm not a poet; I'm a secretary, office of one." Brevoort slows down the pilgrimage along the lonely highway of their grief and meditates on the ineffable nature of their bond. Whether they realize it or not, the playwright finds poetry in their stories. Somewhere during the ritual, we begin to see Elvis ourselves, transubstantiated out of the impassioned longing for the love song that saves us from the fate of being ordinary, from the loving savior who makes us all feel special. Even if, ordinarily, you ain't nothin' but a hound dog.

Jordan Harrison

Claire, in Jordan Harrison's **FIT FOR FEET**, is a good haggler, but she gets more than she bargained for in her betrothed, Jimmy. Earthbound, mall-bound, Claire has chosen for her mate a predictable above-average bourgeois dolt. In the days leading up to their nuptials, Jimmy defies his own predestined orbit and inhabits instead another sphere and time. In the fulfillment of his dream persona, he takes flight—with the confidence and élan, if not the trajectory, of Nijinsky. Claire's materialistic world is 100 percent replaceable; she looks to insurance to cover any losses. Unlike her mother, who has learned to squint at the unpleasant and flirt with what is outside her reach, Claire only accepts the future that resembles her past. And yet...and yet...Claire is gradually seduced by this new man in her bed with "God in my prick." Though she may follow Jimmy, she cannot, or will not fly with him. Instead of joining him aloft in V formation she roughly shakes him from his dream. When finally Claire wakes from her own bourgeois trance, it's too late. Her Nijinsky has leapt out of her reach.

Melanie Marnich

Melanie Marnich's play **THE RIGHT TO REMAIN** operates just a degree or two south of normal. If the volume were turned down just a notch, one would never surmise that the asparagus was overcooked, never mind that the couple's long-time marriage will end when the dishes are done. The drama is only secondarily about the discovery of Peter's infidelity; the power of the play derives from the wooden complacency of his wife and son's reaction. Part of Peter's punishment is the relent- less normalcy to which he's subjected. The audience is caught in an embarrassing denouement whose needs are all pro forma. His son, Josh, has seen through his father's alibi of courting the new snowmobile account. Peter's marriage is about to end with all the spectacle of one of those snowmobiles banking into a deep snow- drift. Once Peter confesses the last digit of his girlfriend's phone number, the mat- ter is settled; the family can begin to digest other important matters, such as the main course of roast chicken. The integers in the phone number click into place dispassionately like the tumblers in a bank vault. There are no bursts of passion or jealousy or pleas for forgiveness to play out—no calls to or for mercy. The play's kitchen-table drama was over before it started, and that foregone conclusion expresses both its matter-of-fact pathos and its rich food for thought.

Susan Miller

In a new warp on an old galaxy, it's the mother who runs away in Susan Miller's **GRAND DESIGN**, as two aging atoms from a nuclear family split into their own orbits. Miller's mother, Frances, is on the move in a trajectory redolent of James Taylor's '70s lyric "Never been there, but I gotta go." Some delayed-reaction human entropy seems to have kicked in. The ultimate destination on Frances' itin- erary may be to go home again, but first she must redefine what it means for two people who care so deeply for each other to part. There's a desperate romantic yearning to define themselves, each other, to encapsulate the world around them. Josh is assembling a time capsule of our culture, our beliefs, our customs, our race. He appears to have appointed himself the curator of our little universe. It might prove easier to get a hold on the entire human race than on one's own personal identity.

Frances left the front porch, the kitchen, the barbecue somewhere in the last century and seems to be searching for a place outside of and irrelevant to time, where a new transcendental hearth may burn. When most mothers and sons have gone their separate ways, these two remain bonded, perhaps even more so when they're apart. Their bond is attenuated by space but hardly severed. In their long-distance confessions and interrogations, mother and son come closer to understanding each other. They also make inroads on why family members are sometimes closest when physically far apart, heading not for a collision in the kitchen but for that telescope onto the heart only distance can bring into focus.

Joe Pintauro

The piping hot meat of Joe Pintauro's **TEN-DOLLAR DRINKS** is served up with a round of high-octane cocktails in a *scène à faire* between two thirty-something actresses. The pair have long comforted and supported each other through the vicissitudes of survival in the same theatre company, but the muscle of their friendship is marbled with the tense, twisted gristle of competition. As the celebrity gods would have it, one of them is tapped for a major movie role that blithely catapults an Oscar onto her mantel. The long suffering friend, Bete, feels betrayed and abandoned and is determined to call her old friend to account by demanding recognition. The Oscar winner, fittingly named Star, realizes she has become the bearer of all the cumulative rejections and humiliations Bete has ever suffered from any and all sources—not a few from Star herself. In high Bette Davis style, Star half dares and half invites Bete to publicly humiliate her in this paparazzi-infested watering hole, offering her million-dollar face as a target for a ten-dollar drink—like some kind of carnival attraction, "Dunk the Star!" The hurled drink hits the bull's-eye, quenching Bete's rage, purging her anger toward her friend, and—if only temporarily—settling the score against time and fame.

John Ford Noonan

John Ford Noonan will never be mistaken for a Tony voter, nor for an establishment dramatist, one of those chaps who regularly beams down the pristine linened dais of nonprofit gala benefits at his gathered fellow elites. Should he turn up with-

out an official invitation, the artistic director would immediately display his direc-
torial prowess by directing security to toss him out a back door. Noonan is not a
presentable writer. One cannot advertise his presence and expect the Rockefellers
to attend. Can there be a better reason to heed his every iconoclastic word?

The forceps that distorted Gino's head at birth earned Noonan's character in
THE RAUNCHY DAME IN THE CHINESE RAINCOAT a lifetime of *non
grata* status at West Hollywood bars and diners. Noonan plays out honor and sin-
cerity as a form of social logic. Super-glue one layer of personal bonding to another of personal sacrifice and eventually (so say the Masons) you produce a rock solid
friendship no mere meteorite can mar. Except if you are simply laminating a lie at
its core. That core wrapped in Oriental tapestries—and tricked out in Bukowski-
esque petticoats—finally radiates its deceit like a gleaming knife.

Noonan is like a knife, too, one of the sharpest, most imaginative dramatists of
his generation. His intelligent pugilism, one step ahead of the rest of us, knocks the
stuffing out of our black-tie assumptions about culture and power.

Woman at a Threshold, Beckoning

John Guare

2

John Guare

John Guare is the Obie and New York Drama Critics Circle Award-winning playwright of such plays as *The House of Blue Leaves, Six Degrees of Separation*, for which he also wrote the screenplay, *Landscape of the Body, A Few Stout Individuals*, as well as his Oscar-nominated screenplay for Louis Malle's *Atlantic City*. He won a Tony Award for his libretto to the musical *Two Gentlemen of Verona* and was nominated for a Tony for his libretto to *Sweet Smell of Success*. His adaptation of *His Girl Friday* premiered to great acclaim at London's National Theatre in 2005. He co-edits the *Lincoln Center Theater Review*, teaches playwriting at the Yale School of Drama, is a council member of the Dramatists Guild, a trustee of PEN America, and received the 2004 Gold Medal in Drama from the American Academy of Arts and Letters.

[*A Line of people who will play* JURORS, ASSISTANT DISTRICT ATTORNEYS, VENDORS, DETECTIVES, GUARDS. *One steps out.* JOHN.]

JOHN [*To us.*] I had been called to Grand Jury duty. Not jury duty but Grand Jury duty.

JUDGE —which is not about finding people innocent or guilty. The Grand Jury determines whether there is sufficient evidence to bring the case to a jury trial. Twenty-three jurors. Alternates in case there's not a quorum—12 votes are needed to indict. Are there any people who cannot serve at this time?

JOHN [*To* JUDGE.] I can't come now.

JUDGE The reason?

JOHN It's not convenient. I'm busy. No reason.

[*To us.*] It was May, 2002. I wanted to enjoy the spring. To see the seasons turn. I wanted to get out of winter.

JUDGE That's your reason?

JOHN I've been working hard. I hoped to have time off.

JUDGE Then we'll call you in December. You should be rested by then. But this is your last extension. You won't be able to get out of grand jury duty in December.

JOHN For the entire month of December?

JUDGE The entire month.

JOHN [*To us.*] So I took now. I got sworn into grand jury along with twenty-two others.

ASSISTANT D.A. Twenty-three jurors. Alternates in case there's not a quorum. Twelve votes are needed to indict.

JUROR #1   Even though some judge had said a prosecutor could get a grand jury to indict a ham sandwich.

JOHN   We did indict. Ham sandwiches aside, we voted for the next three days to indict every case that was brought before us. They were all the same.

ASST. D.A.   I present a case to you of three counts violating Article Eighteen of the Criminal Code and the Interstate Commerce Act in which Miguel Santero sold heroin to undercover agent Ladka. Do any of you know any of the participants in this operation?

JUROR #1   I should hope not.

[JURORS *murmur negative.*]

ASST. D.A.   What proof did you have when you made the arrest?

DETECTIVE   I was wearing a wire—

JOHN   [*To us.*] When the detective left, we could ask the assistant D.A. questions.

JUROR #2   Why does Interstate commerce come into it?

ASST. D.A.   That's a very good question. Since the alleged perpetrator was carrying a gun at the time of the arrest and since no guns are manufactured in the state of New York, it is fair to infer that the weapon was carried into the state over state lines, thereby violating the rules of Interstate Commerce. Any more questions?

JUROR #2   Could this be a setup?

ASST. D.A.   That's a very good question but—for what reason?

JUROR #2   The arresting detective is trying to make himself look good.

ASST. D.A.   I don't think this is relevant to—

JUROR #2   It happened on *Law and Order*.

JUROR #3   I saw that!

JUROR #1   Or the man sold drugs because he needed money for a sick child.

JUROR #3   Extenuating circumstances!

ASST. D.A.   Your job is not to solve a crime or re-enact episodes of *Law and Order* or re-create *Les Miserables*. That's why you don't get to see the person who broke the law. You get me, the assistant district attorney, providing you with hard evidence of whether or not this person should be tried in a court of law. I'll go out of the room and let you vote.

JOHN   [*To us.*] He left.

JUROR #3   I don't like these detectives wearing wires.

JUROR #2   Suppose it was a set up? It's just what happened on *Law and* –

JOHN   [*Impatient.*] That's not for us to decide. The trial will decide that.

JUROR #1   What are you in a hurry for? We got no place to go for a month.

JOHN   Let's vote.

[*To us.*] Didn't my fellow jurors have anything better to do with their lives?

JUROR #1   [*An accusation.*] Ham sandwich.

JOHN   But then what did I have better to do with my life? Over and over, the foreman of our jury would ask for a true bill, meaning is it worth sending to trial.

FOREMAN OF JURY   How many vote for a true bill?

[*Hands raise.* FOREMAN *counts.*]

Eighteen. Nineteen. Twenty one two twenty three. Bring in the D A. We have a true bill.

JOHN [*To us.*] And the ham sandwiches kept coming. Buy and bust. Buy and bust—drug deals—set up drug deals—buy and bust—how many votes for a true bill?

[*All hands go up.*]

All hands went up, day after day, over and over. We got maybe three cases in the morning, three or four in the afternoon. A month of this? God.

ASST. D.A. Lunch break. Be back at two o'clock.

JOHN Most of all, I hated lunch break because the first day I walked around to stretch my legs and find a sandwich. I crossed Foley Square, past City Hall over by Fulton Street. Sandwiches surely over there. Broadway. Wall Street. I came to a long line of people and a lot of vendors selling T-shirts.

VENDOR #1 Proud to be an American.

VENDOR #2 Americans are like the flag—we don't run.

VENDOR #3 We will never forget you.

[THE OTHERS *form a line.*]

JOHN What's this line?

VENDOR #1 To see Ground Zero.

JOHN It's down there?

[*To us.*] I felt a pang. I had never come down here since that day—you know the day. I lived about a mile away from Ground Zero, I guess at Ground One. I saw it all happen that day. I'm still sickened by it—no, not sickened—I'm numbed by it. I still can't look at a picture of that day—or anything on the TV. I turn away or turn off. I knew people who died. Who didn't?—if you were a New Yorker.

JUROR #2 I heard some psychologist say on the radio—NPR—that anyone who witnessed the events of that day will never recover from them.

JOHN Never recover? No big deal. I'm no different from anyone else. I was just one of the thousands who saw those horrific sights first hand. So go stand in line. See it now. Put it into perspective. Maybe this was why I was called to jury duty. To face up to my inner nausea and finally confront Ground Zero and get over it. Put it behind me. Make it history. I tried to get in line.

PERSON IN LINE Hey! Line jumper! Go down to South Street Seaport. Pick up your tickets there like everybody else.

JOHN You need a ticket? Tickets to see Hell? Forget it.

[*To us.*] I went back to the jury room. I took to bringing my lunch every day so I wouldn't be drawn to that line. I didn't want to be tempted to see Ground Zero. It was all right for tourists. Not for me. I still had the smell of those days in my nostrils—was it flesh? I had run into a friend of mine out on the street that night of September 12th who said:

FRIEND Welcome to Auschwitz.

JOHN Here it was May 2002 and that whole catastrophe of last September still made no sense. That pit of Ground Zero was still the abyss of unknowing. I got nauseous, paralyzed remembering it. And now you picked up tickets to see it? Back to reality. Back to Grand Jury—buy and bust—

[THE JURY *forms.*]

ASST. D.A. I present a case to you of three counts violating Article Eighteen of the Criminal Code and the Interstate Commerce Act in which Herman Ramirez sold heroin to undercover agent Ladka. Do any of you know any of the participants in this operation?

[*An* ARAB WOMAN *appears, followed by a* GUARD. *She wears an Arab headdress with her prison garb. She is handcuffed.*]

JOHN [*To us.*] And then one day the door opened and an Arab woman came in, dressed in pants that looked like—were they prison pants? From the waist up, she wore a shawl drawn up over her head framing her face. She looked at all of us. She had a beautiful smile. She was handcuffed from behind. The guard behind her steered her to a chair. The guard undid her handcuffs. He bid her sit down. She turned once before she sat. She did not sit down directly. She turned and then sat. She made a complete circle and then sat down. Did she pause for a moment? Did she look at me? He replaced the handcuffs on one wrist, attaching the other cuff to the arm of the wooden chair. All of us—we jurors who had not been instructed or prepared for this—looked at each other.

JUROR #1 [*Whispering.*] Who is she?

JUROR #2 Why aren't they telling us anything?

[*Another* ASSISTANT D.A. *comes into the room, followed by a* TRANSLATOR *in a business suit.*]

JOHN The Assistant D.A. came into the room, followed by a man who would act as the translator. He sat by her. The Assistant D.A. did not swear her in, in the usual way. She stood. She raised her hand. The translator said something in Arabic to her. She nodded. The assistant D.A. began his questioning. The court stenographer began typing.

ASST. D.A. You understand that your attorney is outside this room. Should you have anything to ask him, you are allowed to leave the room to talk to him.

JOHN The translator leaned into her and whispered softly.

[THE WOMAN *nods yes.*]

ASST. D.A. Would you indicate for the stenographer that the witness said yes?

TRANSLATOR [*Always matter of fact.*] Yes.

ASST. D.A. In 1997, when you first arrived in America, you lived in Jersey City.

[THE TRANSLATOR *leans into her. She listens and nods. All of these transactions will happen very quickly.*]

TRANSLATOR Yes.

ASST. D.A. Who did you live with?

[THE TRANSLATOR *leans into her. She whispers to him.*]

TRANSLATOR With my ex-husband's cousin. A distant relative.

ASST. D.A. How long did you live there?

[THE TRANSLATOR *leans into her. She whispers to him.*]

THE TRANSLATOR Less than a month.

ASST. D.A. The address?

[THE TRANSLATOR *leans into her. She whispers to him.*]

TRANSLATOR I do not remember the address.

[THE ARAB WOMAN *looks out at* JOHN.]

JOHN She looked up into the room. She looked at me.

ASST. D.A. You moved to Brooklyn with your ex-husband's parents for less than a month. Can you tell us the address?

[THE TRANSLATOR *leans into her. She whispers to him.*]

TRANSLATOR I do not remember the address.

ASST. D.A. Then back to Jersey City. To the same household?

[THE TRANSLATOR *leans into her. She whispers to him.*]

TRANSLATOR No. To a girl friend and her children for two months.

[THE ARAB WOMAN *looks out at* JOHN.]

JOHN She did it again. Right at me.

ASST. D.A. Can you tell us the address?

[THE TRANSLATOR *leans into her. She whispers to him.*]

TRANSLATOR I do not remember the address.

ASST. D.A. Then to Chicago, Illinois with a cousin named Zaccariah Abdullah and his wife Fatima for two months.

[THE TRANSLATOR *leans into her. She whispers to him.*]

TRANSLATOR Yes.

[THE ARAB WOMAN *looks out at* JOHN.]

JOHN And again. Her lips moved. What was she saying to me?

ASST. D.A. Can you tell us the address?

[THE TRANSLATOR *leans into her. She whispers to him.*]

TRANSLATOR I do not remember the address.

ASST. D.A. With your ex-husband's relative, did you ever discuss acts of terrorism?

[THE TRANSLATOR *leans into her. She whispers to him.*]

TRANSLATOR No.

ASST. D.A. Did you ever discuss terrorism with your Chicago relatives?

[THE TRANSLATOR *leans into her. She whispers to him.*]

TRANSLATOR No.

ASST. D.A. What did you do for money between 1997 and 1999?

[THE TRANSLATOR *leans into her. She whispers to him.*]

TRANSLATOR Family support. No welfare.

ASST. D.A. What identity do you use?

[THE TRANSLATOR *leans into her. She whispers to him.*]

TRANSLATOR Egyptian passport the only I.D.

JOHN Egypt? I sat up. I had been to Egypt. Was she looking at me because she recognized me? Had I met her?

ASST. D.A. We have a list of every number you called from Federal Detention Center. Do you recognize the following telephone numbers?

[THE ASSISTANT D.A. *passes her papers. She looks at them.* THE TRANSLATOR *leans into her. She whispers to him.*]

TRANSLATOR Yes.

ASST. D.A. Who are they?

[THE TRANSLATOR *leans into her. She whispers to him.*]

TRANSLATOR   Cousins. Friends.

ASST. D.A.   Have you ever discussed acts of terrorism with any of these people?

[THE TRANSLATOR *leans into her. She whispers to him.*]

TRANSLATOR   No.

ASST. D.A.   Have you planned acts of terrorism?

[THE TRANSLATOR *leans into her. She whispers to him.*]

TRANSLATOR   No.

ASST. D.A.   Who do you know in Detroit?

[THE TRANSLATOR *leans into her. She whispers to him.*]

TRANSLATOR   My cousin.

ASST. D.A.   Have you ever talked to your ex-husband in code?

[THE TRANSLATOR *leans into her. She whispers to him.*]

TRANSLATOR   No, only normal talking.

ASST. D.A.   When did you first hear about jihad?

[THE TRANSLATOR *leans into her. She whispers to him.*]

TRANSLATOR   Don't recall.

ASST. D.A.   How do you understand *jihad?*

[THE TRANSLATOR *leans into her. She whispers to him.*]

TRANSLATOR   *Jihad* is the struggle for women against temptation, against family and raising children properly.

[THE ARAB WOMAN *looks out at* JOHN.]

JOHN   She looked at me again. Was it pleading?

ASST. D.A.   You told INS agents you had never heard of jihad until after September 11th·

[THE TRANSLATOR *leans into her. She whispers to him.*]

TRANSLATOR   The imam at the mosque told me what had happened September 11th was not jihad.

ASST. D.A.   Did you ever think of seeking revenge against the United States for convicting your ex-husband?

[THE TRANSLATOR *leans into her. She whispers to him.*]

TRANSLATOR   No.

ASST. D.A.   Have you read the Koran?

[THE TRANSLATOR *leans into her. She whispers to him.*]

TRANSLATOR   Yes.

ASST. D.A.   Have you taught Islam?

[THE TRANSLATOR *leans into her. She whispers to him.*]

TRANSLATOR   In Jersey City to a group of women every Saturday.

ASST. D.A.   Did you teach other concepts of *jihad?*

[THE TRANSLATOR *leans into her. She whispers to him.*]

TRANSLATOR   No.

[THE ARAB WOMAN *looks out at* JOHN.]

JOHN   I couldn't get close enough. What was going on in her mind?

ASST. D.A.   Do you know anyone who's committed acts of terrorism, other than your husband and his cousin?

[THE TRANSLATOR *leans into her. She whispers to him.*]

TRANSLATOR   No.

ASST. D.A.   Did you ever plan to commit terrorism?

[THE TRANSLATOR *leans into her. She whispers to him.*]

TRANSLATOR   No.

ASST. D.A.   Did you ever discuss with another person how to commit acts of terrorism?

[THE TRANSLATOR *leans into her. She whispers to him.*]

TRANSLATOR   She wants to see her lawyer.

ASST. D.A.   Let the minutes reflect the witness is leaving the room to consult with her attorney.

JOHN   The guard came into the room, unlocked her handcuffs. She stood up. She made that turning motion. She looked at me. She smiled. The guard shackled her again. They left the room.

[THE WOMAN *and her* GUARD *leave.*]

We went berserk.

JUROR #3   Is she a terrorist?

JUROR #2   What are the charges?

JUROR #1   Is this one of those unconstitutional Ashcroft things? Is she one of thousands of Arabs being held illegally? Let her go!

JUROR #3   I say Hang her!

ASST. D.A.   Calm down. It's part of a long-term investigation. But one thing. She seems to be looking out into the room. I didn't ask, but could anyone on the jury conceivably know her? Has anybody here been to the Middle East?

JOHN [*To us.*] I decided to keep my mouth shut.

ASST. D.A. Anyone? No one. We are hearing testimony from a material witness that might be brought to the trial jury. We are here not merely to witness her testimony but to probe the case, to go deeper, or to provide a new angle. You, the grand jury, by witnessing and certifying her testimony are helping us do the job of investigating the attacks on September 11th as well as embassy bombings in Kenya and Tanzania.

JUROR#1 Who is she?

ASST. D.A. Not important.

JOHN It is!

ASST. D.A. She is Narima Abdullah. She is 32 years old. She is Egyptian—married Mustapha Norur who's presently incarcerated—

JOHN [*To us.*] She came to America illegally in 1997. She went to Canada in 1999 hoping to get legal status there until she could apply for U.S. legal residence. She applied for asylum in Canada as a single mother. She was told it was easier to bring a child from Egypt to Canada for protective custody which was denied. She came back to America in 2001 but she can't remember the name of the month.

JUROR #2 Can't remember the month! Give me a break.

JOHN By any chance, was she in Egypt in 1996?

ASST. D.A. That's a very good question. I have no idea. Why?

JOHN Just wondering.

JUROR #1 Her ex-husband?

ASST. D.A. Her ex-husband applied in 1998 for temporary protective status but as he was involved in holy war, he was accused and convicted. She is testifying on promise of immunity.

The only charge so far that can be brought against her is perjury which carries a five- to ten- year sentence for each charge of perjury.

JOHN Is she a terrorist?

ASST. D.A. That's a very good question—

JOHN The Assistant D A started to speak. But the door opened.

[THE WOMAN *and* THE GUARD *return.*]

She held up her hands. He unlocked the cuffs. And again she made that circle. She turned very slowly, very gracefully, looked at me—just for a second—as she sat down in the chair—to which he shackled her again. Had I met this woman in Egypt?

ASST. D.A. I'll repeat my question. Did you ever discuss with another person how to commit acts of terrorism?

[THE TRANSLATOR *leans into her. She whispers.*]

TRANSLATOR No.

JUROR #3 She's lying.

JUROR #2 Through the teeth.

ASST. D.A. Now let me enter document #1.

JOHN [*To us.*] The Assistant D A held up large photos so we could see them. They were mug shots of Arab men.

ASST. D.A. Do you recognize any of the people in these photos?

JOHN   She looked at each face.

[THE TRANSLATOR *leans into her. She whispers to him.*]

TRANSLATOR   No. I do not know these people.

JOHN   [*To us.*] Then we gasped.

ASST. D.A.   Do you recognize this man?

JOHN   [*To us.*] The Assistant D.A. then held up a photo of Mohammed Atta, the pilot of the first plane to crash into the Trade Center.

[THE TRANSLATOR *leans into her. She whispers to him.*]

TRANSLATOR   No. I do not know this man.

JOHN   But we all recognized the face. We all knew who he was. The whole world knew who he was.

JUROR #3   I say Hang her.

ASST. D.A.   You had a computer and an email address. What chatrooms did you visit?

[THE TRANSLATOR *leans into her. She whispers to him.*]

TRANSLATOR   "Maktoud."

ASST. D.A.   The purpose of that site?

[THE TRANSLATOR *leans into her. She whispers to him.*]

TRANSLATOR   People make jokes in Arabic.

JUROR #2   That I'd like to hear.

JUROR #3   So this Ayatollah came into a bar—

ASST. D.A.   "Islam Way"?

[THE TRANSLATOR *leans into her. She whispers to him.*]

TRANSLATOR   It is a way of reciting the Koran online.

JUROR #3   Oh sure. "*Faster Pussycat Kill Kill* dot com."

ASST. D.A.   On a sheet of paper that was found on your person when you were taken into custody, you've written Revolution.com. Let me admit into evidence document #2.

[THE TRANSLATOR *leans into her. she whispers to him.*]

TRANSLATOR   It is the name of a game I copied down for my son to play in Egypt. May I say something?

[THE TRANSLATOR *leans into her. she whispers to him.*]

TRANSLATOR   Mrs Abdullah wants to rectify something. She recognized the photo of the last man as the man responsible for the first crash. She only meant that she did not know him personally.

JOHN   I had seen that smile. My wife and I had gone on a holiday to Egypt for my 50th birthday. I wanted something special, something as ancient as me was our joke. We even had a friend in Cairo who had once lived in New York and said if you're ever in Cairo. We visited him. Wonderful knowing a local in Cairo. Our last night there, our friend took us to a part of the city where tourists did not usually go. The city instead of slums began to be decorated with large bolts of white cloth with Arabic designs in red or green painted on them. The city was transformed like a stage set. Drums started playing. What was happening? You'll see, our friend said. You'll see.

We walked and walked through the decorated city. I saw people spinning—men and women wearing white costumes and odd pointy hats spinning on one foot, their left foot—their hands outstretched—beatific smiles on their faces. We saw a man spinning with a snake around his neck, then another man, then a dozen men spinning each with a snake around his neck. My friend said proudly: This is what I wanted you to see. Happy birthday. It was a convention, a conference of whirling dervishes. Ten thousand dervishes who live around the Muslim world were congregating in Cairo.

It was terrifying. We saw people shooting out balls of colored paper hung over the street on wires. We walked through mobs. Is it safe? It was not safe, but we could not leave. Thousands of people dancing with these beatific smiles on their sublime faces, whirling to this hypnotic passionate music. Music of a few notes for a passionate purpose. Then I saw this woman. When I passed, the whirling woman—her—Mrs. Abdullah—suddenly stopped, looked at me and beckoned me. She made a slow beckoning gesture. I turned around. No one was there. I looked at her. Me? She nodded. I moved towards her. My wife pulled me back. When I turned again, the woman—Mrs. Abdullah—was gone and now here she was. I stood up in the jury room.

[*Cries out.*] I know this woman!

[JOHN *advances on* THE WOMAN.]

JOHN   Were you involved in 9/11?

WOMAN   Yes.

JOHN   [*To us.*] I would crack this case. I would supply a meaning to the events of that terrible day when the world spun out of control.

[*To* THE WOMAN.] Were whirling dervishes involved?

WOMAN   We were all dervishes.

JOHN   What is the purpose of the spinning?

[THE TRANSLATOR *leans into her. She whispers to him.*]

TRANSLATOR To see God. Yes. She remembers you.

JOHN I thought dervishes were peaceful.

WOMAN We are. It was not a plot of terror. It was a plot of conversion to bring our message of joy to the western world, to have us all be finally One, living in peace.

JOHN Peace?

WOMAN We all want peace. The planes that day were spinning as we headed to the towers. The people inside those planes were spinning in ecstasy. When the spinning planes hit the towers, the people within the towers began spinning ecstatically. The ones who died were taken to paradise. The ones who survived were those who refused the word. They will be sent out into the world never to spin again. They had their chance. It was like Adam and Eve. God offered them the chance to find transcendent peace by spinning. They refused God's joy. That's the sin of Eden. God sent them out of Eden never to spin again. God came again on September 11th to give us a second chance. This was the second coming—the chance to achieve ecstasy.

JOHN Is conversion too late now?

[THE TRANSLATOR *leans into her. She whispers to him.*]

TRANSLATOR No! God is merciful. God will show us the way.

JOHN By spinning?

[THE TRANSLATOR *leans into her. She whispers to him.*]

TRANSLATOR Yes.

JOHN How do I do it?

[THE TRANSLATOR *leans into her. She whispers to him.*]

TRANSLATOR You spin on your left foot, your arms outstretched. You think of God. You chant.

JOHN If I get dizzy?

WOMAN That's the world trying to hold you back. "Dervish" means threshold.

JOHN "Dervish" means threshold?

WOMAN You are walking into a new consciousness.

JOHN It's like the hokey pokey—only to God.

[THE TRANSLATOR *leans into her. She whispers to him.*]

TRANSLATOR What is hokey pokey?

JOHN I'm on the wrong side of the threshold. I'm trying to make a joke. That's what we do on the wrong side of the threshold. I want to cross that threshold.

WOMAN You shall.

[*She makes a beckoning gesture.*]

JOHN That day. It was all spinning and ecstasy?

WOMAN Yes.

JOHN I had seen the towers crumble. Did they spin as they toppled? Was there a spinning motion?

WOMAN Yes.

JOHN I saw the planes spinning. I saw the buildings whirling. Like you that night in Cairo.

WOMAN Like me. "Dervish" means threshold. I'm on the threshold. Come join me.

[JOHN *and* THE WOMAN *begin to spin.*]

JOHN That day was Allah taking us to a new threshold, a new way of life?

WOMAN Yes.

JOHN Not anguish, not terror, but joy?

WOMAN Yes.

JOHN Is this possible?

[To us.]

I know it's not possible but is it possible just to rethink it? That all those thousands of people that day did not die in terror, but rather were—*struck* by a moment of ecstasy. People leaping from the towers in ecstasy—spinning as they plunged down. All those whirling people shown the truth. Finding God.

WOMAN That's right. You know the truth. Keep spinning. Don't stop.

[JOHN *stops.*]

JOHN You're crazy.

WOMAN You're the one making me up.

JOHN I'm looking for an answer.

WOMAN To what?

JOHN To this numbness I feel—

WOMAN You've made me up and you call me crazy?

ASST. D.A. Excuse me—A juror in the back row seems to be standing and trying to say something. Are you all right?

JOHN [*Dazed.*] Oh. I'm sorry. I was just standing. Yes—standing is what they call this. Not spinning. I'm sorry.

[*To us.*] My fellow jurors all looked at me, some cross, some puzzled. The woman next to me passed me a bottle of water. "Thank you thank you—a momentary dizziness." I sat. The questioning resumed.

ASST. D.A. You sought temporary protective status in the U.S. claiming fear of returning to Egypt.

[THE TRANSLATOR *leans into her. She whispers to him.*]

TRANSLATOR My ex-husband wrote that on an application seeking asylum in Canada.

ASST. D.A. You feared return to Egypt?

[THE TRANSLATOR *leans into her. She whispers to him.*]

TRANSLATOR Yes.

ASST. D.A. Fear of what?

[THE TRANSLATOR *leans into her. She whispers to him.*]

TRANSLATOR Hardship. No work. Nothing else.

ASST. D.A. Not because of your former husband's conviction?

[THE TRANSLATOR *leans into her. She whispers to him.*]

TRANSLATOR Yes. They will question me why I divorced him. But I do not fear returning to Egypt now.

ASST. D.A. Why?

[THE TRANSLATOR *leans into her. She whispers to him.*]

TRANSLATOR Because my family told me I had no reason to fear.

ASST. D.A.   But before September 11th, you did have reason to fear?

[THE TRANSLATOR *leans into her. She whispers to him.*]

TRANSLATOR   Yes.

ASST. D.A.   Why?

[THE TRANSLATOR *leans into her. She whispers to him.*]

TRANSLATOR   Circumstances in Egypt make life very difficult. Life itself. We feared prosecution because our government is not to be trusted.

ASST. D.A.   Now you do trust it?

[THE TRANSLATOR *leans into her. She whispers to him.*]

TRANSLATOR   We trust the government now.

ASST. D.A.   Why?

[THE TRANSLATOR *leans into her. She whispers to him.*]

TRANSLATOR   My family tranquilized me.

ASST. D.A.   In Canada you said you feared execution if you returned.

[THE TRANSLATOR *leans into her. She whispers to him.*]

TRANSLATOR   I don't recall that.

ASST. D.A.   Thank you very much.

JOHN   The guard approached her and unlocked the cuff on the arm of the chair. She stood. She extended her wrists. He clamped on the other cuff. She held her wrists to her mouth. She started to make that slow spinning gesture. The guard led her out of the room. She did not look at any of us. She smiled. She was gone.

[THE ARAB WOMAN *and her* GUARD *are gone.*]

JUROR #1   Will we see her again?

JUROR #2   Will she be deported?

JUROR #3   Where do they send her?

ASST. D.A.   Those are all very good questions. You never know. We split up these investigations so people tracking her can never tell what it is we're looking for.

JOHN   What did you learn today?

ASST. D.A.   A very good question. I just collect the data. Other people put it together. Next case. Three counts in violation of Article 18 of the Criminal Code. Possession of illegal substances—

JOHN   We returned to "buy and bust."

FOREMAN   We've heard the evidence. Vote for a true bill?

[THE JURORS *raise their hands.*]

Unanimous.

JOHN   She didn't come back the next day. Nor the next. But all of us are still here. The month goes on. Hearing evidence. Buy or bust. Buy or bust. No answers. No judgments.

I thought of the dervishes. Spinning spinning to see God.

I looked them up on Google dot com. Part of Sufi. Not really for me.

They say we can't go back to living the way we did. But where do we go? What do we do? Living with that pit at Ground Zero that won't ever go away no matter how much redevelopment they do, no matter how many competitions they hold, the pit that's inside us as much as in Lower Manhattan won't ever go away because it's always been there. September 11th didn't make the terror. It showed us what we've always known is there. I'm embarrassed to ask this question. How do we get to God? Is that even a sensible question? I think of the terror of that day. How do we reach its mirror image? The polar opposite of that horror must be ecstasy. Where is the ecstasy? Is finding that ecstasy the only way to get out of this numbness, this grief—this fear—

What is that woman's truth? How can anyone know what her truth is? How can we know what happens on *any* day?

ASST. D.A.   Next case. Two counts of a violation of article 18—

FOREMAN   Vote for a true bill? Hands up? Twenty-one—twenty-two.

[THE ARAB WOMAN *appears, beckoning to* JOHN.]

JOHN   I raised my hand.

[JOHN *beckons to the* WOMAN.]

• • •

The
Grand Design

Susan Miller

Susan Miller

Susan Miller won The Susan Smith Blackburn Prize and The 2004 Pinter Review Prize in Drama for her play, *A Map of Doubt and Rescue*, which was done in workshop by New York Stage and Film and The Ojai Playwrights Conference. She holds a Guggenheim Fellowship in Playwriting and two OBIE awards for *Nasty Rumors And Final Remarks* and her acclaimed one person play, *My Left Breast*, which premiered in Actors Theatre of Louisville's Humana Festival, and which has been performed in theatres across the U.S., Canada, and Europe. Other plays: *For Dear Life, Flux, Cross Country, Confessions of a Female Disorder, It's Our Town, Too, Arts and Leisure,* and *Sweeping the Nation.* Her plays have been produced by Second Stage, The Public Theatre, Naked Angels, the Mark Taper Forum, Trinity Rep. and the O'Neill Playwrights Conference among others. Miller was a Consulting Producer on the first season of the Showtime series, *The L Word.* She is a member of the Dramatists Guild. For more information on the author and her work: www.susanmillerplaywright.com.

characters

JOSH   Late 30s. Smart. Underlying (and not so underlying) angst. Governed by his questions—the joy and difficulty of what he searches for and what he finds—and an abiding sense of humor.

FRANCES   Josh's mother. Late 50s/early 60s. Whatever her son has—trace it back! She is also, like him, in the process of discovery.

Their rhythms are bantering, intimate, passionate.

2–3 PEOPLE   Any gender. Diverse. They sit somewhere on the periphery of the stage almost as if watching the action until they become part of it.

time

The present.

· · · production note · · ·

There are 3 Slides shown at the beginning of the play. And 1 Slide near the end. I include the illustrations from which to make the slides at the end of the script. With a minor adjustment of words in the opening, the play can be done <u>without</u> the use of slides.

The play can also be (and has been) performed without the "chorus" of other Actors by assigning their words to Josh and Frances.

· · · production history · · ·

The Grand Design was staged in Los Angeles at the Canon Theatre in an evening of original one-act plays benefiting Cure Autism Now, starring Lily Tomlin and Eric Stoltz, directed by Robert Egan. It was also performed by Marsha Mason and Scott Cohen at Town Hall in New York for Brave New World, a marathon of plays commemorating 9/11.

The Grand Design was produced by City Theatre of Miami and was a finalist for the Actor's Theatre of Louisville's Heideman Award.

• • •

[*Lights up. JOSH paces, then leans against a desk for ballast. He relishes talking about what he knows and what he struggles to know. A slide goes up. This is not a lecture. It's an inquiry. An expedition. He is working something out as he talks. In front of us. With us.*]

JOSH   The first page of the Dutil-Dumas message, sent from a transmitter in the Ukraine. To signal other civilizations. The message was encoded using a system called Lincos that starts with simple mathematical ideas and builds to complex information about who we are.

[*Beat.*]

In case there's anyone out there.

[*Another slide.*]

April 5th, 1973. Pioneer 11 is launched into deep space, carrying a message in the form of a six-by-nine inch gold plaque showing human figures, Earth's location in the universe, and a diagram of the hydrogen atom.

[*Beat.*]

In that same year, on the day before Pioneer 11 makes its voyage, the ribbon is cut on the tallest building in the world. 110 stories high on sixteen acres in lower Manhattan. "A living representation," according to the architect, "of man's belief in the cooperation of men…and through this cooperation his ability to find greatness."

[*Another slide.*]

November 16th, 1974. The Arecibo Observatory in Puerto Rico
sent this message toward a cluster of stars 25,000 light years
away. A string of 1,679 bits or ones and zeros, it can be assem-
bled into a pictogram showing the figure of a man, a telescope,
the numbers, DNA, and the solar system.

[*End slides.*]

1977. My personal favorite: gold plated LPs—remember
phonograph records? LPs in aluminum cases. Launched on
board Voyager I and II. With, of course, instructions on how
to play the records.

[*He breaks into a dance to a lush arrangement of Sinatra. After a few
bars, the music stops. Then, suddenly:*]

JOSH Items missing from Voyager, Dutil-Dumas, Arecibo, and all
previous messages that have traveled through space and time:
The Sign over Auschwitz. ARBEIT MACHT FREI. Work
makes one free. A slave ship carrying the first of 50 million
people Africa will lose to slavery or death, en route. The hole in
our ozone layer. A small woman refusing to sit at the back of the
bus. Yen. Francs. Dollars. Money.

[*A blank slide goes up.*]

JOSH 2005. What? What the fuck's the message this time?

[*A woman, FRANCES, his mother, speaks to the audience from another part of the
stage.*]

FRANCES My son is kind of a poet scientist. He's got this grant to
come up with a message for alien civilizations. To let them know

who we are. The human race. He's hit a wall. And I've left town.
On foot.

JOSH My mother is walking. She's walking with no clear purpose all
across the United States. It's her response to the—situation. To
turning a certain age. To my breakup. It's her memorial to the
nature of our times.

[*Beat.*]

She calls me from the road.

FRANCES I'm on the Eleanor Roosevelt Trail.

[*A succession of calls.*]

I'm standing outside a church on top of a hill in Ohio where the
Underground Railroad connected.

[*Beat.*]

I don't know where I am. But, I see cows.

I'm covering ground. I'm walking past the things I know.

I met this person who picks the places to stop along the way. You
know when you get directions—on your computer. What's that
called—map something? Well, they actually send people out to
find interesting things to do along the routes. I just never
thought of that. There are all kinds of jobs I never thought
about.

JOSH Look, I'm sorry. I'm sorry things didn't work out and I didn't give
you grandchildren and—

FRANCES [*To audience.*] He thinks I'm out here because he failed in his
marriage. I'm out here because I failed. To know what to do next.
I was sad. And I started walking. I was walking in circles all

around the house. Finally, I just took it outside. And I'm not the only one out here. There are mothers walking all over the place.

[*Beat.*]

I'm worried he won't find love.

[*The phone rings in his house. Although they begin talking to each other, as if on the phone, this is dropped shortly and they just address each other directly.*]

FRANCES Hi, Sweetie!

JOSH Mom? Where are you?

FRANCES If I wanted to be located, I would stay home.

JOSH Are you just walking aimlessly or do you have some kind of plan?

FRANCES I do have a plan. To walk aimlessly. All right, the story so far. I just had pie. They use shortening and whole eggs and I don't care. Because while I eat my pie and have my coffee, I'm not drowning in the facts. There is no true history of the United States. I am not guilty. I am not wanting. I am not disappointed. So, how are you coming with your memo to alien civilizations?

JOSH See, when you say it like that—

FRANCES Like what?

JOSH Like how you said it.

FRANCES Like how I said memo or how's it coming?

JOSH How you said it like you had no opinion or no opinion you'd be ready to reveal, even though we can be pretty sure that you are always in possession of an opinion. Anyhow, I'm not writing a memo. It's more like an equation. You know? Which lays out the thing to be discovered or proven. It's not necessarily what we are—it's what we could be.

FRANCES [*Struck.*] That's lovely.

JOSH For a lie, you mean.

FRANCES Maybe it's a lie we need.

JOSH Well, I do, I guess. I need it.

[*Beat.*]

See, the big discoveries—gravity, particle theory, chaos, DNA—they place us. They put us in the physical world. But they're just descriptions. Of our physical properties. Our propensities. What we're capable of—what's possible, what we've already accomplished, I mean how do you—first … I thought, well, fucking, of course. Sexual congress. For them to see how we do it and how much we like to do it. But, fucking causes so much confusion and anxiety. And what if they interpret two figures expressing their ardor as some kind of cruel rite? And the truth is, fucking doesn't last. And, then, what about madness, disorders of the mind, bodies that aren't whole?

[*Beat.*]

I should just tell them to be human is to impose yourself on the world. This is how I see it, so this is how it is.

FRANCES

[*A beat.*]

Or—you could take this grant money and give it away to actual people. So they could eat, go to school, and maybe collectively expand and redefine the concept of what it is to be human.

JOSH Okay, sister, listen, didn't I give up my beautiful SUV when you were on your moral imperative not to drive big gas guzzling automobiles thus entrenching us in a relationship with oil producing nations and consequently undermining what we tout to be our own unique position of being free in the world?

FRANCES   I was quoting. I didn't come up with that myself, which is disturbing, because I don't always see how things fit and I'm always completely thrown to learn there's this relationship between a simple thing like buying a car or a carton of milk and the decline of civilization.

JOSH   Well, just put your two cents in about this, would you, and help me out here. I mean, is it sentimental to think there's something—anything—we have in common with everyone else on earth?

FRANCES   What everyone wants to know is who am I going to be? And then, who am I going to be with who'll make it not so terrible to *be* me. And if you have children, well, who are they going to be and who are they going to be with and will I like who they are and who they're with and how do I keep them safe?

[*Beat.*]

Maybe you're reaching, Josh. Maybe the story of one person is all they need to know about us.

JOSH   Where the hell are you?

FRANCES   In my tent.

JOSH   You are not in any kind of a tent.

FRANCES   In my tent outside of my room at the motel. You don't think I'd really pee in the open, do you? You should go outside. It is an alarmingly beautiful night.

JOSH I can't go outside. I can't think outside.

FRANCES Did you open my letter yet?

JOSH [*Avoiding.*] I haven't had a chance—actually.

FRANCES I know you're carrying it around in your pocket and it's getting smushed and I need you to read it.

JOSH I know you want me to read it, Frances. So it must be important. And that, of course, brings up my morbid fear of important letters.

FRANCES Josh.

JOSH And I don't really have the time right now.

FRANCES [*Retreating.*] Okay.

JOSH I'm in over my head with this thing.

FRANCES Look, if the aliens have a sense of humor, they'll see the irony. Or they'll receive it like the French do when you try to speak in their language.

[*A beat.*]

Tell me…just show me what you've got so far.

JOSH Just—you know, I'm still working on it.

[*After a moment, an ACTOR steps forward from another part of the stage and stands with arms outstretched—or JOSH manipulates him into this position, framed by the light of the slide projections, to represent a living slide show of JOSH's work in progress.*]

JOSH That we're—incomplete. That we long for. That we miss our chances. And we're born to repeat: If only. If only!

[*A second ACTOR comes forward and joins hands with the first.*]

FRANCES   How it is to hold someone else's life in your own.

[*Beat.*]

Can you add a dog? I think we need them, somehow.

[*The* ACTOR *holds the other in his arms, as if he were wounded or ailing, in need.*]

JOSH   That we're moved. That we can meet another person's sorrow or subjugation with an answering cry and a wish to make it better. Not because we're thinking, "that could be me" but because that is me.

[*Beat.*]

You know, if you put a group of six-month-old babies in a room and one starts to cry, pretty soon they all start crying. They can't differentiate. They are all one living, breathing, wailing, sobbing, suffering being.

[*Another* ACTOR *joins them. they stand still. only their expressions change, illustrating different reactions to something we don't see.*]

JOSH   The chemistry of the brain changes with certain events. Once you witness an atrocity—or hear a cruel remark. When you cause the disappointment in someone's eyes. Or see an act of courage. There's a shift. Now your brain's accommodating this new information. You're still pulled to the earth by gravity. And your blood type is still O-positive. But what happens to other people is placing itself in your cells. It resides in you now. And you're not the same. It changes you forever.

[*The actors move to the rear of the stage, where they sit.*]

FRANCES   Come outside. Be with me, tonight.

[*After a moment, he walks "outside." They both stand under a starry sky.* JOSH *looks up toward the heavens, addressing the unknown civilizations.*]

JOSH   Okay, I have some questions for *you*! Do you have pets? Do you marry? Is there gender? Does it matter to you if another of your species, group, tribe, community, has different markings? Do you have prisons? Are you kind? Do you sleep? Do you have mothers?

FRANCES   [*Joins him in shouting out to the universe.*] This is who we are! Hurtling through time, tumbling, stretching, moving through time to what we're meant to be. This is us. Becoming!

[*Beat—to Josh.*]

Please open the envelope.

JOSH   [*A moment.*]

Fine.

[*He retrieves the letter from his pocket and opens it.*]

JOSH   I see something that looks like a house. And little stick figures in crayon.

FRANCES   The other side.

[*He turns it over and starts to read out loud.*]

JOSH   The last will and testament of—[*as he realizes what it is*]—my one and only mother! Jesus. I don't want to see this. I don't want to think about it.

FRANCES   Well, you have to.

JOSH   Why? Why do I have to? I don't have to.

FRANCES   You're my executor, beneficiary, and medical proxy. And when you have children—

JOSH Would you please—with the children.

FRANCES It could happen.

JOSH Are you all right? Should I be worried? I'm worried.

FRANCES I'm fine. It's just something a person has to do. I'm all right.

[*A beat. As Josh looks over the will. And turns it over.*]

JOSH So, what's this drawing?

FRANCES Something you did as a child. You drew a house. Next to other houses. Because you said our house needs those other houses. So you drew a house with people inside. Small people. And big people to take care of them, to give them an example, to accompany them on their way.

[*Beat.*]

My god, you were so—[*As it comes to her.*] Smart. Josh. What makes us human is other humans.

[*A moment.*]

JOSH [*To audience.*] After my mother dies, some years from now, and I've married my first wife all over again—and a simple child's drawing has gone into space—I tell my daughter the story of one person. Walking. Looking at things. Listening to other people's stories. Wanting to know.

[*He turns back to Frances. They are on their phones again.*]

FRANCES [*So full, it can be understated.*] I love you, Josh. I love you so much.

[*The slide of Josh's childhood drawing goes up.*]

OTHER ACTORS [*Each speaks a line in turn.*] In Wonder. In Awe. In Loss. In Gratitude. In Sympathy. In Release. In Pain. In Memory. In Celebration. In Mourning. In Difficulty. In our Stumble and Fall. In each Attempt. In Remission. In Rapture. In the Beginning. In the End. In IT.

JOSH

[*Beat.*]

I love you, too, mom.

[*The light narrows to frame the drawing. Until, lights fade.*]

. . .

Blue Moon Over Memphis: A Noh Drama about Elvis Presley

Deborah Brevoort

Deborah Brevoort

Deborah Brevoort lived for many years in Alaska before moving to New York City. She is the author of *The Women of Lockerbie*, which won the silver medal in the Onassis International Playwriting competition and the Kennedy Center Fund for New American Plays award. It is published by Dramatists Play Service and was produced off-Broadway by the New Group and Women's Project in 2003 and at the Orange Tree in London in 2005. She is the librettist of *King Island Christmas*, with composer David Friedman, which has been produced all over the U.S. and Australia. Deborah also wrote the book and lyrics for *Coyote Goes Salmon Fishing*, a musical with composer Scott Richards, which won the Frederick Loewe Award. *Signs of Life*, a comedy about faith and doubt, was a gold medalist in the Pinter Review's Prize for Drama. Other works include *The Poetry of Pizza*, a comedy about love, *The Blue-Sky Boys*, an all-male comedy about NASA's Apollo engineers, (commissioned by the EST/Alfred P. Sloan Foundation Science & Technology project), *Into the Fire*, set in Alaska, (published by Samuel French) and *Goodbye My Island*, a musical tragedy inspired by events in Alaskan history, with composer David Friedman. She is currently writing *The Velvet Weapon*, a political farce about the Velvet Revolution in Czechoslovakia. Deborah was one of the original company members of the Perseverance Theatre in Alaska and is an alumnus of New Dramatists. Her website addresses are *www.DeborahBrevoort.com* and *www.kingislandchristmas.com*.

··· A few notes about ···
Noh Drama and Elvis Presley
before reading
Blue Moon Over Memphis

Noh drama is a highly stylized form of Japanese theatre that is based on music, dance and gesture. The written text in a Noh drama is only one thread in a tightly woven performance fabric made up of many threads. In order to create a Noh performance of *Blue Moon Over Memphis* a visual, musical and gestural text needs to be developed to accompany the written text.

Noh drama is a form of theatre that lacks most of the dramatic conventions we expect in a play in the west, such as plot, action, or character development. Instead, Noh is meditative theatre and the aim of a Noh play is to explore, poetically and rhythmically, a single emotion over the course of several hours.

Noh dramas are based on stories that are well known to the audience. There is the appearance of a ghost of a famous dead person in just about every Noh play. The text of a Noh drama is inspired by poetry that is also well known to the audience. Noh is often called the "theatre of reminiscence," because there is a looking back in just about every play.

I decided to write a Noh play about Elvis Presley because I was searching for a way to bring this meditative form of drama into the American theatre. I kept asking myself what story did we have that everyone would know—and know so well that I wouldn't have to tell it? What famous dead person would we want to see? What music, dance and poetry traditions did we have that would enable us to look back and remember? What is our form of meditation and what could I put on the stage that would enable an American audience to enter the meditative state?

I found my answer in pop culture, because it is the only culture that all people in America share by virtue of the fact that it invades everyone's homes and cars through radio and television. Elvis is the King of pop culture: his music is still played on radio stations across the country, sales of Elvis paraphernalia continue to skyrocket, and the number of Elvis fans continue to grow—not to mention Elvis sightings which are reported weekly in the nation's tabloids. I realized that Elvis was the perfect Noh subject when I sat down to listen to his love songs, for what I thought was the first time. When I turned on the tape player, I was surprised to discover that I already knew them. The journey I took when I listened to his music approached the meditative state of Noh drama. I realized that oldies music in general, and Elvis songs in particular, are an American form of meditation, and one of our ways of "looking back."

Blue Moon Over Memphis attempts to engage an American audience by combining familiar music, dance and story elements with theatre conventions that are unfamiliar. It is not necessary for the audience to understand Noh in order to understand the play. In fact, *Blue Moon Over Memphis* relies on the audience not knowing the form. However, it is necessary for the director, designers and actors working on the play to understand the Noh form thoroughly in order to build an American production upon its conventions.

Although *Blue Moon Over Memphis* is written in a traditional Noh structure, it is not my intention that it be performed as Japanese Noh with Japanese costumes, sets, gestures and music. Rather, the production of the play should be completely American. The text of *Blue Moon Over Memphis* takes the poetic conventions of Noh, collides them with an American story, and spins them into a distinctly American context. It is my intention that the conventions of Noh be spun into their American contexts as well.

One final note. Even though Noh can be pretty highbrow stuff, *Blue Moon Over Memphis* was not written for a highbrow audience. On the contrary, it was written for the consumers of pop culture who rarely set foot in the theatre.

Deborah Brevoort

Since writing *Blue Moon Over Memphis*, I've had the opportunity to direct two student workshops of the play (one at Brown University and the other at the New School University's Eugene Lang College) and to see it presented in readings and workshops by different directors. Since Noh drama is foreign to most American theatre artists, and because my text was written with specific conventions in mind, I have added additional notes in the back of this script to assist those considering a production of the play in the future. I have also added stage directions to give the reader some indication of where these elements accompany the text. The directions are minimal, and don't explain how the elements should work but they will hopefully provide the reader with an image of what a contemporary Elvis Noh drama should look like on the stage.

Deborah Brevoort

persons

JUDY An Elvis Presley fan. Forty years old [waki].

> [*Please note: The role of* JUDY *should be played by two actresses—one who is silent and moves through the play, and one who sits on a bench and recites* JUDY's *lines from the side or back of the stage.*]

THE MAN A heavyset black man in his 40s, wearing a white "Las Vegas Elvis"-style pantsuit [mae-jite].

OSCAR The groundskeeper at Graceland [kyogen].

ELVIS As a young man, dressed in a gold lamé suit [nochi-jite].

THE CHORUS (6 total) consisting of two groups [one female, one male] who are on stage for the duration of the play: **THE FANS**—A group of three women who never enter the Meditation Garden and **THE MEMPHIS MAFIA**—Three of Elvis's bodyguards.

KOKEN [Noh Stagehand] A man or woman who is on stage at all times.

set

On the back wall of the stage is a stylized painting of a tree. The tree could be a magnolia or dogwood tree, or some other tree found in the American South. Upstage right is a bridge leading off stage.

time

The anniversary of Elvis's death.

location

The Meditation Garden at Graceland where Elvis is buried.

Note on Setting: The set for a Noh drama does not contain any realistic depiction of location or place. This is established by the words and movements of the actors, and also by a few stylized objects brought on stage at different times by the Koken. Some of the objects called for in this play, which should not be of realistic size or proportion, are:

The Music Gate: the famous wrought-iron gate that stands at the main entrance of Graceland. It is ornamented on each side with musical notes and figures of Elvis playing the guitar. **Elvis's Grave**: marked by his motto "TCB" pierced by a lightning bolt. (TCB stands for "Taking Care of Business.") **The Eternal Flame**: which burns at the foot of his grave.

· · ·

[*Before the play begins,* THE MEMPHIS MAFIA *should be positioned around the theatre guarding the stage as the audience enters and takes their seats. The* KOKEN *can be setting props, sweeping, doing sound and light checks, etc., to prepare for the performance just like a stage manager or concert technician might do.*]

[*Once the audience is seated,* MEMPHIS MAFIA #1 *should check his watch then give a nonverbal go-ahead to the* KOKEN *that it is time to begin.*]

KOKEN [*To the actors.*] Places!

> [THE MEMPHIS MAFIA *take their places on stage.* THE FANS *enter and take their places on the bridge. The* KOKEN *brings in the eternal flame and sets it on the grave, then takes his or her place on stage.*]
>
> [*The two* JUDYs *enter on the bridge. They should be dressed identically and should walk slowly in unison, in the traditional Noh manner.*]

FANS [*In unison.*] Tomorrow is August 16th, the anniversary of Elvis's death. My name is Judy. I'm from Cleveland, Ohio. I am only one of the thousands of fans who are traveling to Graceland to mourn the death of The King. I'm driving to Memphis tonight. If I leave Cleveland at dusk, I'll get there by dawn.

I've never been to Graceland before. It's a trip I've always wanted to make. It's now or never. I'm 40 years old, I'm not getting younger.

I fill my thermos with coffee and leave Cleveland at rush hour. I sit in traffic and head for the open road. My dream trip to Graceland doesn't begin until the moon rises before me on the highway and I leave the city behind.

[*The two* JUDY*s split. The one who will speak the role will sit on a bench on stage, and the other will continue the journey to Graceland, walking around the stage in a circular Noh pattern using occasional abstracted "driving" gestures.*]

JUDY   I take I-71 to Louisville Kentucky
Then 65 south to Nashville Tennessee
I pick up 40 in Nashville
and head west into Memphis
I do 70 all the way

JUDY   [*Continued.*]

The moon is my only companion
as I drive alone down the lonely highway
I pretend the moon is my lover
I daydream the whole night away

On Rt. 40 as day is approaching
I roll down my window to hold onto the night
I keep my eye on the sun risin' fast in the rearview
I watch the moon fade and slip out of sight

JUDY   I arrive in Memphis at daybreak.

[JUDY *takes a step and turns.*]

JUDY   Here I am, in Memphis. I check into a motel with ten-dollar rooms. I sleep straight through the day.

[*Pause.*]

JUDY   I awaken at dusk, as the day goes to sleep. I watch from my window as the evening sky turns from blue to black. When the moon rises high over the neon, I leave my room. I check out of the motel. I drive south, to Graceland, on the outskirts of Memphis.

[JUDY *takes another step and turns.*]

JUDY   And here I am, at Graceland. I'm standing before The Gate. Look! There it is! For real!

[JUDY *points. The stage is empty. Pause. Then, the* KOKEN *brings some representation of the Music Gate on stage.*]

JUDY   The Gate, The Gate
The Music Gate!
With a Blue Moon shining over it!

[THE FANS *enter the stage from the bridge, walking in silence in a candlelight procession.* FAN 1 *begins to whisper the following words.* FANS 2 *and* 3 *join in. These words should not be spoken in unison. They should overlap.*]

FANS   There's a Blue Moon Over Memphis tonight!
Look at the blue moon! Shining above!
Blue Moon Over Memphis
Bring back the one we love!

[THE FANS *address* JUDY.]

FAN 1   I come to Graceland every year. Before Elvis died, I came every day. I stood at The Gate for ten years. There was something I wanted to tell him, but I never got the chance.

JUDY   I tried to write him letters. I could never find the words for what I had to say.

FAN 1   I'll never forget the first time I saw him.

FAN 2 He was driving his Cadillac, dressed in a jacket the color of sky.

FAN 3 He rolled down the window, lowered his sunglasses, smiled at me and winked.

FAN 1 Then he laid a patch of rubber and went screeching through The Gate.

JUDY I saw him once, in concert. He walked out on stage and stood before the mic. He stood there five minutes, he didn't make a move. [*Pause.*] Then, he hit his guitar and broke all the strings.

FAN 2 Every time I saw him, chills ran up my back.

JUDY Whenever he sang a love song, I felt he was singing to me.

FAN 3 I keep a lock of his hair in a locket around my neck.

JUDY I have a thorn from a rose he threw into the crowd. I keep it with me all the time.

[THE KOKEN *brings a candle to* FAN 1 *who in turn gives it to* JUDY.]

FAN 1 Here's a candle for the all-night vigil.

FAN 2 It was lit from the flame on his grave.

FAN 3 Don't let it go out.

FAN 2 Keep it going through the night.

JUDY When will they open The Gate and let us inside?

FAN 1 They won't. They don't let anyone into the Meditation Garden after dark.

JUDY Why not!

FAN 1 Look around you. What do you see?

[JUDY *looks out over the audience.*]

JUDY   People. Miles and miles of people.

FAN 1   That's right. Too many people.

JUDY   But...I drove all this way! I came to sit beside his grave at the hour of his death!

FAN 1   So did everyone else.

JUDY   You don't understand...

FAN 1   No, I do.

FAN 2   You feel like you're special.

FAN 3   Like you should be the exception.

FAN 2   Everyone feels like they're special.

FAN 3   There are ten thousand fans here tonight who feel like they're special.

FAN 1   Ten thousand fans who feel just the same as you.

[*Begin: The Fan Dance, which is danced by* FAN 1 *using abstracted* ELVIS FAN *gestures while the others speak:*]

FAN 2   There's the Fan from Denver Colorado
who worked day shift at the Bowling Alley
and drove all night
like you
just to sit beside his grave

FAN 3   The Fan who flew from Boston Massachusetts
and took two vacation days
from the Accounting Firm
Just to stand outside The Gate

FAN 2   There's the Fan from Tulsa Oklahoma
who left dinner in the micro
for her husband
and caught the 2:15 to Memphis
on Amtrak #9

FAN 3   The Fan who will stand at The Gate
until morning
When she catches the 10:11 back home

FAN 2   There's the Fan from Phoenix Arizona
who takes phone orders for Sears & Roebuck

FAN 3   and called in sick
so the boss wouldn't dock her pay

FAN 2   The Fan who hitchhiked from Montana
in the back of a pickup
and has to wait at The Gate until dawn

MEMPHIS MAFIA 1   There's the Fan from Wheeling West Virginia

MEMPHIS MAFIA 2   The Fan from Nashville Tennessee

MEMPHIS MAFIA 3   The Fan from Utah

MEMPHIS MAFIA 1   Wyoming

MEMPHIS MAFIA 2   California

MEMPHIS MAFIA 3   New Hampshire

FAN 2   who won't get to kneel beside his grave

FAN 1   There's the Fan
who walked to Graceland
from Georgia
and still waits outside The Gate.

[*Pause.*]

MEMPHIS MAFIA 1   You can go in tomorrow.

FAN 1   During the day.

FAN 2   They'll let you pass the grave, quickly, in a line.

FAN   They won't let you stop.

MEMPHIS MAFIA 2   There are guards along the way.

[THE FANS *move to the side of the stage and assume the choral position.*]

JUDY   I thought if I sat beside his grave, under the light of the blue
moon, I would find those words I've always wanted to say.

   [JUDY *looks down at her candle, then up at the moon.*]

JUDY   But maybe I'm just fooling myself
   I am not a poet
   I was never any good with words
   I'm a secretary
   I answer the telephone at the insurance company
   I work in an office of one
   I'm forty years old
   I don't have a husband
   I don't have a lover
   I eat my dinners alone
   I eat at Hojo's on Friday
   I eat at Denny's on Saturday
   I spend my evenings at home,
   listening to Oldies Radio
   I spend my evenings alone,
   looking out the window
   I spend my evenings alone,

singing love songs
to no one in particular.

[THE MAN, *a heavyset black man in his late 40s appears on the bridge, walking in the traditional Noh manner. He wears a white polyester pantsuit in the style of "Las Vegas Elvis."*]

THE MAN   Who was singin' that song?

[JUDY*'s reverie is broken.*]

JUDY   Hmmm?

THE MAN   Were you the one singin' that song?

JUDY   What song?

THE MAN   [*Sings.*] "Time goes by so slowly..."

JUDY   I don't know. I might have been. I was thinking it.

THE MAN   It's my favorite song.

JUDY   It's my favorite song, too.

THE MAN   Kinda stirs up your loneliness, don't it?

JUDY   Yes, it does.

[THE MAN *opens The Music Gate.*]

THE MAN   Well, come on in, darlin'. Don't sit out there all by your lonesome.

JUDY   You mean...?!

THE MAN   Uh-huhn.

JUDY   Oh, WOW! Oh, Thank you!

THE MAN Shhhhh!

JUDY Oh, sorry!

MAN I don't want the others to see! [*Whispers.*] Come on in! Hurry on through!

[JUDY *slips through The Music Gate.*]

THE MAN It's just that you can't be too careful with these fans. They can get outta hand in a flash. I seen 'em do things you wouldn't believe.

[THE KOKEN *removes The Music Gate.*]

THE MAN I seen 'em

MEMPHIS MAFIA 1 pick all the grass from the lawn 'till there was nothin' left but dirt.

THE MAN I seen 'em.

MEMPHIS MAFIA 2 pluck one of the trees clean of all its leaves.

THE MAN They

MEMPHIS MAFIA 3 steal lawn chairs from the pool and light bulbs from the lamps.

MEMPHIS MAFIA 1 They chip paint off the house and pull nails from the fence.

MEMPHIS MAFIA 2 The day of the funeral, they were stretched on the lawn like corpses.

MEMPHIS MAFIA 3 They were droppin' ever' which way like flies.

MEMPHIS MAFIA 1 One fan threw herself on the flame, nearly burned herself to death.

MEMPHIS MAFIA 2   One tried to climb in the casket.

MEMPHIS MAFIA 3   Even today, some try to dig up the body.

JUDY   You've seen fans do all those things?

THE MAN: All those things, and more.

> [*Pause.* JUDY *looks around.*]

JUDY   Where's the Meditation Garden?

THE MAN   You're in it.

JUDY   And the grave?

THE MAN   Right here.

> [*The* KOKEN *brings the TCB Grave Marker.* JUDY *kneels before it.*]

THE MAN   Here
    Under the Marble
    Under the flame that burns eternal
    Under the lightning bolt
    his emblem
    and TCB
    his motto
    lies
    Elvis Presley
    The American Man
    Dead
    but still Taking Care of Business

> [*Pause.*]

THE MAN   So you're a fan, huh? A dyed-in-the-wool, true-blue Elvis Presley fan?

JUDY   Yes. I've been a fan all my life.

THE MAN   Which Elvis Presley did you like?

JUDY   There was only one.

THE MAN   Oh no, there were many.

[Begin: The Dance of Many Elvises, which is danced by THE MAN *using abstracted Elvis gestures and poses.]*

MEMPHIS MAFIA 2   There was the Elvis from Tupelo
        the Mississippi white boy
        who sang like a negro
        and played broom stick for guitar

FAN 2   the boy with the funny hair
        who came from white trash
        and didn't have shoes

MEMPHIS MAFIA 1   There was Elvis the Pelvis
        who mimicked the preachers
        and turned hellfire and damnation
        into "Good Rockin' Tonight"

FAN 1   who moved his hips while singing gospel
        and sang hymns with his eyes closed in church

FAN 3   There was Elvis
        the Sensuous Cyclone
        who clutched the mic
        and looked at girls with lidded eyes

MEMPHIS MAFIA 3   who grinned and sneered
        and twitched his leg
        and brought out the National Guard

MEMPHIS MAFIA 2   Elvis
who snapped guitar strings
like they were made of cooked spaghetti

FAN 3   whose voice flowed like thick syrup
on warm autumn days

FAN 1   Whose voice was softer than velvet
Softer than kisses
Sweeter than soft bites
on the neck

MEMPHIS MAFIA 3   There was the boy who was sent to the Army

FAN 2   And got his hair cut
while millions watched and wept

THE MAN   [*Salutes.*] Private Presley

FANS 1, 2 and 3   Number 533-1076-1

FAN 1   There was Elvis of Hollywood
the star of twenty-seven movies

MEMPHIS MAFIA 2   most of them bad

FAN 2   Elvis
who staged his own comeback
when everyone said he was dead.

FAN 3   There's the man they called "Fire Eyes"

FAN 1   And the man they called "Memphis Flash"

MEMPHIS MAFIA 3 The man who studded
the buckle on the bible belt
with diamonds
after turning it into gold

FAN 2 There's the man who threw scarves
to the crowd
and gave Cadillacs to strangers

THE MAN The man who had to sing with clenched fists
so fans wouldn't steal his rings

MEMPHIS MAFIA 1 The man who didn't own the rights to his
own face

THE MAN The man
who grew tired of being Elvis Presley
and died one night
from an overdose of drugs.

JUDY There's another Elvis. An Elvis you didn't mention.

THE MAN Which Elvis is that?

JUDY The lonely Elvis. The Elvis who walked a lonely street.

THE MAN: You know about that Elvis?

JUDY That's the Elvis I know best of all.

THE MAN That Elvis is not buried here.

JUDY Where is he buried?

[THE MAN *holds out his hand.* THE KOKEN *brings him his white scarf, which he takes and hangs around his neck.* THE MAN *begins to walk slowly in a circular Noh pattern in the traditional Noh manner.*]

THE MAN I lie

MEMPHIS MAFIA 1 in the hearts of lonely people

MEMPHIS MAFIA 2 who walk alone down lonely streets.

THE MAN I roam

MEMPHIS MAFIA 3 restless, in the night sky

MEMPHIS MAFIA 1 and live in the light of the moon.

THE MAN I live

MEMPHIS MAFIA 2 on the tops of lonely mountains

MEMPHIS MAFIA 3 and circle high in the sky on spread wings.

MEMPHIS MAFIA 1 I live in the candle that is lit at dinners for one.

MEMPHIS MAFIA 2 I live in radios that play all night in dark rooms

MEMPHIS MAFIA 3 and in televisions that fill

MEMPHIS MAFIA 1 empty houses with sound.

[THE MAN *arrives back at center stage next to* JUDY.]

MEMPHIS MAFIA 2 I am Elvis.

THE MAN Elvis

MEMPHIS MAFIA 3 the Blue Moon Boy

MEMPHIS MAFIA 1 who sits staring out the window.

MEMPHIS MAFIA 2 I have not yet found my resting place.

THE MAN He has not yet found his resting place.

MEMPHIS MAFIA 3 The lonely never do.

THE MAN The lonely never do.

JUDY You knew him well then?

THE MAN I knew him as well as you can know anyone.

JUDY: Tell me...who are you? What is your name?

[THE MAN *turns and walks slowly towards the bridge.*]

MEMPHIS MAFIA 1   Under the lightning bolt
In the Meditation Garden
On the night of the Blue Moon

THE MAN   The Man disappears.

[THE MAN *drops his white scarf on the ground.* THE FANS, JUDY *(speaking) and* JUDY *(moving) all turn their heads suddenly and stare at the fallen scarf.* THE MAN *walks slowly over the bridge and exits.*]

[THE FANS *follow* THE MAN. *They stop at the end of the bridge and remain facing off stage where* THE MAN *has disappeared, their backs to the stage and the audience.*]

[THE KOKEN *checks his or her watch, then tosses three Budweiser Beer cans to the* MEMPHIS MAFIA. THE KOKEN *exits over the bridge, walking at a normal pace like a concert technician, pushing his or her way through* THE FANS *who still stand watching offstage where* THE MAN *has disappeared.*]

[JUDY*(moving) joins* JUDY *(speaking) on the bench. They sit in the shadows along the edge of the Meditation Garden.*]

[THE MEMPHIS MAFIA *leave the choral position and sit along the edge of the stage, as if they are now "on break." Perhaps one of them lights a cigarette. When they pop the tops to their beer cans,* OSCAR, *the Groundskeeper, enters in a flurry, bursting through* THE FANS *and running over the bridge onto the stage, trampling the white scarf as he enters. He pulls a garbage can on wheels, and carries a broom and a dustpan-on-a-stick.*]

OSCAR   Oh, lordy. Oh, lordy.

FANS We want Elvis! We want Elvis!

OSCAR Oh lordy. Oh lordy.

FANS We want Elvis!

OSCAR I thought I'd seen everything but this one beats all!

[OSCAR *yells at* THE FANS.]

OSCAR [*Yells.*] Ladies, really!

This is no way to behave!

FANS We want Elvis! We want Elvis!

OSCAR Oh lordy. What am I going to do? There are ten thousand
women out there, who think they've seen Elvis! Just now!
Walkin' around Graceland! They're goin' wild! They're takin' off
their panties and tossin' 'em in the air! Ten thousand women!
Ten thousand panties! Right there on Elvis Presley Boulevard!
Why, it looks like a snowstorm in the middle of August!

FANS We want Elvis! We want Elvis!

OSCAR [*Yells.*] Ladies!
You're seein' things!
Elvis is dead!
He's not walkin' around!

FANS We want Elvis! We want Elvis!

OSCAR [*Yells.*] He's dead, I tell you!
D-E-A-D Dead!
I know! I buried him myself!

FANS We want Elvis! We want Elvis!

OSCAR They don't believe me! They think he's alive! [OSCAR *watches* *the* FANS.] Oh lordy, what a sight! A full moon in the sky and ten thousand on the ground! If this wasn't Graceland, I'd think I was dreaming.

OSCAR [*Yells.*] Ladies! Please!
I beg of you!
Put your pants on!

FANS We want Elvis! We want Elvis!

OSCAR Oh lordy. I gotta sit down. Old Oscar's gotta sit down.

[OSCAR *sits on* ELVIS's *grave. He pulls a pair of white panties out of his pocket and mops his brow.*]

OSCAR Just between you 'n me, folks, I don't get it. I been the groundskeeper here for 30 years and I just can't figure out what all the fuss over Elvis is about. So, the guy twitched a leg! I can twitch a leg!

[OSCAR *stands up and twitches his leg.*]

OSCAR And he shook his hips! Well, I can shake my hips!

[OSCAR *shakes his hips.*]

OSCAR And then, he gets a double chin and puts on a belly! Well, I've got three chins and a belly! But the women aren't fallin' over me!

[OSCAR *dances on* ELVIS's *grave—badly imitating* ELVIS.]

OSCAR What's he got that I don't?

[OSCAR *sits back down.*]

OSCAR You know, when he gained all that weight, I thought he was finished. Especially when the newspapers called him "Elvis Rock 'n Roly Poly Presley!" I mean, the guy was Fat 'n Forty! What could be worse than that? But, sure as I'm sittin' here, it didn't make any difference! The women went just as wild as ever. And then, when he died...

[OSCAR *looks around and lowers his voice.*]

OSCAR ...well, just between you 'n me, folks, I was glad! I know that's a terrible thing to say, but I thought there would finally be a chance for the rest of us fellas! But do you think bein' dead made any difference? Not on your life! The women continued to go wild! And they're still goin' wild today! Over a corpse! Over a stiff! I mean, the guy is dead! He's been six-feet-under, in the grave, for 15 years! And just look at 'em out there! You figure it out!

FANS We want Elvis! We want Elvis!

OSCAR [*Yells.*] Ladies!
Please!
Give old Oscar a break!

FANS We want Elvis!

OSCAR [*Yells.*] How many times do I have to tell you! He's not here!

FANS Yes he is!

OSCAR [*Yells.*] No he's not!

FANS We saw him!

OSCAR [*Yells.*] You couldn't have seen him! He's DEAD!

[OSCAR *falls to the ground and beats it in frustration.*]

OSCAR And that's another thing. These women who see him all over the place, eating hamburgers and hot dogs in Houston and pizza in Portland and donuts in Detroit! I don't get it! Elvis is dead! How can he be walkin' around eatin' all those things?

THE FANS We want Elvis! We want Elvis!

OSCAR [*Yells.*] Go to Wisconsin!
He was spotted there last week
Eating cheese!

FANS We want Elvis!

OSCAR Oh lordy. In thirty years of being the groundskeeper here, I never seen nothin' like this!

[OSCAR *mops his brow and looks up at the moon.*]

OSCAR It must be the Blue Moon. Once in a Blue Moon the moon is blue. That must be it.

FANS We want Elvis!

OSCAR I give up.

FANS We want Elvis! We want Elvis!

OSCAR [*Yells.*] All right ladies!
You can have him!

[OSCAR *gets up, wearily.*]

OSCAR Oh lordy, it's going to be a long night...

[OSCAR *sweeps the white scarf into his dustpan.*]

OSCAR All right, ladies
You're right
Elvis is alive
Only he's not here at the moment
He just left
He's on his way downtown
to get a box of jelly donuts
If you leave now you can catch him.

[OSCAR *walks over the bridge, pulling the garbage can behind him. He exits, pushing his way through* THE FANS.]

[*The Meditation Garden is silent and still. There is no movement, except for the eternal flame that flickers, faintly, in the light of the moon.*]

[*The* KOKEN *enters very quietly at the end of the bridge and lights a match.* THE MEMPHIS MAFIA *jump to attention.* MEMPHIS MAFIA 1 *crosses down stage and looks around.*]

MEMPHIS MAFIA 1 Who's there?

FANS [*Whisper in unison.*] Long Live the King!

[*The* KOKEN *lights candles for* THE FANS]

[MEMPHIS MAFIA 2 & 3 *fan out across the stage, on "high alert." The* KOKEN *crosses to the two* JUDYs *sitting on the bench, and lights a candle for* JUDY (*Speaking*). THE MEMPHIS MAFIA *surrounds the bench and confiscates the* KOKEN's *matches.*]

[THE KOKEN *returns to the koken position on stage.* THE MEMPHIS MAFIA *return to the choral position.*]

[*The moon passes slowly behind a cloud.*]

FAN 1 [*Whispers.*] Look! How the night grows darker!

FAN 2 [*Whispers.*] How the flames of our candles burn brighter.

FANS 1, 2, and 3 [*Whispers.*] The hour of his death is approaching.

FAN 1 [*Whispers.*] That fateful hour.

FAN 2 [*Whispers.*] Look! How the moon passes under a cloud!

[*The shadows in the Meditation Garden dance and waver with the passing of the moon.*]

[*The moon reappears.* JUDY *(moving) gets up from the bench and slowly crosses to center stage, looking at the moon as* JUDY *(speaking) speaks.*]

JUDY How pretty it is
     The moon in the night sky
     It makes everything blue
     You don't know if you're awake
     or dreaming

     [JUDY *(speaking) remains on the bench. She watches the moon, then starts to hum softly to herself.*]

[ELVIS *appears on the bridge, walking in the traditional Noh manner. When he steps onto the stage, he performs one of the universally recognized Elvis gestures in slow motion.*]

     [JUDY *(speaking and moving) does not look at* ELVIS, *she looks at the moon.*]

JUDY I must be dreaming
     This is the moment I've been waiting for
     And the moments you wait for
     never seem to come
     except in dreams

ELVIS You ain't dreamin', darlin'
     You're wide awake
     You're sittin' here
     In the Meditation Garden
     at Graceland
     Clear as day
     Under the moon

Talkin' to Elvis

JUDY I talk to Elvis all the time
I talk to Elvis when I'm sleeping
I talk to Elvis when I'm awake
I talk to Elvis at night when I
sit at my window
looking out at the moon
Talking to Elvis doesn't mean
that Elvis is there

ELVIS Well, Elvis is here
You're talkin' to him right now
You're talkin' to him right here
at the foot of his grave

JUDY Really?

ELVIS Really.
Go on
Pinch yourself if you have to
Pinch yourself
so you know it's for real

[JUDY *(speaking and moving) pinches herself and looks at* ELVIS *for the first time.*]

JUDY There you are

ELVIS Here I am

JUDY This is a dream come true.

ELVIS Dream come true, huh?
Lemme tell ya something
about dreams
darlin'

MEMPHIS MAFIA 1   Dreams

MEMPHIS MAFIA 2   is all

MEMPHIS MAFIA 3   there is.

ELVIS   I should know
My whole life was a dream
A dream I didn't wake up from
until I died.

MEMPHIS MAFIA 1   And then?

MEMPHIS MAFIA 2   And then?

JUDY   And then?
What did you find when you woke up in death?

ELVIS   More dreams
Just dreams upon dreams
That's all there is

MEMPHIS MAFIA 1   Dreams

ELVIS   Dreams

MEMPHIS MAFIA 2   Dreams

ELVIS   And loneliness
Dreams and loneliness
in life and death.

JUDY   Loneliness.

ELVIS   Yes. There's loneliness in death, just like there's loneliness in life.
Only in death, you don't got all those things you got in life to fill
your loneliness with. You don't got records

MEMPHIS MAFIA 1   or clothes

MEMPHIS MAFIA 2   or jewelry

MEMPHIS MAFIA 3   or girls.

ELVIS   You don't got televisions

MEMPHIS MAFIA 1   radios

MEMPHIS MAFIA 2   stereos

MEMPHIS MAFIA 3   cars.

ELVIS   You don't got none of those things at all. All you can do to fill the loneliness of death is walk and wander and hope that you find something or someone to take your loneliness away.

JUDY   Do you ever find it?

ELVIS   I ain't come across it yet.

[ELVIS *walks half way around the stage in a circular Noh pattern in the traditional Noh walk as the following is spoken:*]

MEMPHIS MAFIA 1   Like the moon that walks alone across the empty sky

MEMPHIS MAFIA 2   The dead walk also

MEMPHIS MAFIA 3   on a path

MEMPHIS MAFIA 1   that nothing crosses

MEMPHIS MAFIA 2   but mist and fog.

MEMPHIS MAFIA 3   Nothing

MEMPHIS MAFIA 1   Nothing on the path at all

MEMPHIS MAFIA 2   Nothing but emptiness

MEMPHIS MAFIA 3   Emptiness all around.

[ELVIS *arrives back at center stage.*]

ELVIS   Look
at the moon
high
in the empty sky
It's light
in the night
shows
how much
of nothin'
there is

MEMPHIS MAFIA 1   Nothing

MEMPHIS MAFIA 2   Nothing

MEMPHIS MAFIA 3   So much of nothing.

[JUDY *looks at the moon.*]

    ELVIS   You're a lonely soul
ain't ya
sittin' alone like that
alone under the lonely moon
No one to talk to
No one to sit by your side
Just sittin' there
all by your lonesome
singin' love songs
out loud to the moon
I used to sit like you're sittin'
alone at my window
alone under the lonely moon
I spent whole nights

just sittin' like that
just sittin' in the dark
just sittin' at the window
just sittin'
where no one could see me.

[*Begin: The Dance of Loneliness which is danced by* ELVIS *using abstracted* ELVIS *poses and gestures:*]

ELVIS   I'd get so lonely

MEMPHIS MAFIA 1   I'd spend whole nights
doin' nothin'
but sit at the window
and watch the fans
stand at The Gate

ELVIS   I'd get so lonely

MEMPHIS MAFIA 2   I'd spend my nights
lost in daydreams

MEMPHIS MAFIA 3   and my days lost deep
in the dreams of sleep

ELVIS   I'd get so lonely

MEMPHIS MAFIA 1   I'd spend whole days
sittin' at the window
lookin' out on the boulevard

MEMPHIS MAFIA 2   The Elvis Presley Boulevard
named after me

ELVIS   and do nothin'
but watch cars drive by

MEMPHIS MAFIA 3   cars with windows made of glass

MEMPHIS MAFIA 1   not windows made of mirrors

MEMPHIS MAFIA 2   cars I never could have
with clear glass windows
that people could see into

ELVIS   I'd get so lonely

MEMPHIS MAFIA 3   my body would ache

MEMPHIS MAFIA 1   Just ache all over

MEMPHIS MAFIA 2   Ache

MEMPHIS MAFIA 3   with the hunger of loneliness

MEMPHIS MAFIA 1   The hunger that starts in your heart

MEMPHIS MAFIA 2   and spreads into your arms

MEMPHIS MAFIA 3   The hunger that settles over your shoulders
like the touch of a lover
who is gone

ELVIS   I'd get so lonely
I would sit all night
and talk to the moon
and when the moon was gone
I'd talk to myself

MEMPHIS MAFIA 1   Lonely

MEMPHIS MAFIA 2   for the sound of a voice
to fill the silence of the empty room

MEMPHIS MAFIA 3   Lonely

MEMPHIS MAFIA 1   for the sound of a voice
        any voice

ELVIS   even if the voice was my own.

MEMPHIS MAFIA 2   I'd get so lonely bein' alone
        that I'd go out at night
        and wander in the crowd

MEMPHIS MAFIA 3   and then get so lonely
        that I'd go back to my room
        to sit alone again
        at the window

ELVIS   [*Pause.*] You ever get lonesome like that? Lonesome, right in the
        middle of a crowd?

MEMPHIS MAFIA 1   Lonesome

MEMPHIS MAFIA 2   Lonesome

ELVIS   So doggone lonesome? So lonesome you could cry?

JUDY   I've been lonesome like that for most of my life.

ELVIS   Me too.

[*Pause.*]

MEMPHIS MAFIA 1   And now, in death
        I long for the loneliness of life

MEMPHIS MAFIA 2   I long for a window to sit at

MEMPHIS MAFIA 3 There's no windows in the grave
        just darkness and silence
        and the nightly visit of the moon

MEMPHIS MAFIA 1   I spend my death

longing for my lonely window

MEMPHIS MAFIA 2   just longing
for the lonely comforts of
my lonely room

MEMPHIS MAFIA 3   I spend my death
singing lonely love songs

MEMPHIS MAFIA 1   just singing love songs
out loud to the moon.

ELVIS   Like you.

[JUDY *looks at the moon.*]

JUDY   The moon

MEMPHIS MAFIA 2   The moon.

MEMPHIS MAFIA 3   The lonely moon.

ELVIS   Yep. The moon is a lonely companion, darlin'.

[ELVIS *looks at the moon. The* KOKEN *brings a microphone on a stand and sits it center stage, then returns to his or her position. A spotlight comes up on the microphone. There is the thunderous sound of screaming* FANS. ELVIS *stands outside of the circle of light, looking at the microphone fearfully. Finally, he walks into the spotlight.* THE FANS *scream louder. He clutches the microphone, as if to sing.* THE FANS *quiet down; the crowd becomes silent waiting for him to begin. But he doesn't sing. Instead, he speaks directly to the audience.*]

ELVIS   I wonder if you're lonesome tonight like me…

[*He peers beyond the spotlight trying to see the crowd.*]

ELVIS   It's too bright to see you, but I'm sure you must be. You know, it's true that "life is but a stage" and we all play a part. I played your lover, you were my sweetheart. When I stepped into this light, it was love at first sight even though I couldn't see you. I was hidden in the spotlight so you couldn't see me too. Now my life is over, and the stage is empty and bare. I've come back and you'll still there. Darlin, you're still hiding in the darkness, I'm still hiding in the light. Can we ever end this loneliness? Could we end it here tonight?

[*The spotlight fades out.* ELVIS *is left on the empty stage, exposed, without the safety of the spotlight. He looks out at the audience; he can see their faces for the first time. Long pause as he looks. When he can't take it any longer, he turns his back to the audience as if to flee. Then, he begins to exit, walking slowly toward the bridge in the traditional Noh manner.*]

JUDY   Look at the moon.

[THE FANS, MEMPHIS MAFIA *and both* JUDY*s look at the moon.* ELVIS *continues walking slowly.*]

MEMPHIS MAFIA 1   It's leaving the night sky

MEMPHIS MAFIA 2   like a one-night lover fleeing your bed with the morning's first light

MEMPHIS MAFIA 3   A one-night lover who leaves no trace of warmth on your pillow

MEMPHIS MAFIA 1   A one-night lover who leaves no trace of love on your sheets

MEMPHIS MAFIA 2   A one-night lover who leaves no trace of nothing.

MEMPHIS MAFIA 3 Nothing

[ELVIS *stops and turns back to face the stage. He looks up at the moon.*]

ELVIS Nope…nothin'.
Nothin' at all.

[ELVIS *disappears over the bridge.*]

JUDY Elvis? [*Pause*] Elvis? There's something I always wanted to say to you.

FAN 1 The moon is gone

FAN 2 the long night comes quickly to an end

JUDY Elvis? I always wanted to say…

[*She stops. Long pause.*]

FAN 3 She searches the morning sky

FAN 1 for words

FAN 2 that do not come.

[JUDY (*Moving.*) *turns and sees that* ELVIS *is gone.*]

JUDY Elvis?

FAN 1 Elvis?

FAN 2 Elvis?

FAN 3 Elvis?

FAN 1 Elvis?

JUDY [*Moving.*] Elvis?

JUDY [*Speaking.*] Elvis? Where are you? Where have you gone?

[JUDY *turns slowly and faces the audience. The* MEMPHIS MAFIA *leave the choral position and fan out across the stage. They address the audience.*]

MEMPHIS MAFIA 1, 2 and 3   Ladies and Gentlemen

MEMPHIS MAFIA 2   Elvis

MEMPHIS MAFIA 3   has left

MEMPHIS MAFIA 1   the building.

[JUDY *and the* FANS *blow out their candles.*]

[*It is morning. The stage is flooded with light.*]

• • •

··· production notes about ···
Noh Drama and Elvis Presley

A general note about the process of colliding two cultures and exploring a contemporary subject with a theatrical form that is nearly 600 years old. I realized very quickly in the creation of this play that I couldn't simply lift the conventions of Noh and tack them on to the Elvis subject. In the same way that a contemporary poetic drama written in the iambic pentameter of Shakespeare's time would feel false to the language, rhythms and spirit of today, so too would a too-strict adherence to the elements of Noh betray the energy and spirit of Elvis Presley. Instead, I had to examine each convention used in the Noh for what it was designed to achieve for the 14th-century Japanese audience, and then find some equivalent in 20th-century American culture that would do the same for an audience today. That said, there are a few places in the play where I do lift an element straight out of the Noh and apply it to Elvis, but in each of these cases, it is always done with a clear eye to how that element will work in an American context and be perceived by an audience who is unfamiliar with it.

For example: it didn't make sense to use the traditional Noh weeping and sitting gestures in the play because they would confuse an American audience, and not reveal anything about Elvis who had plenty of his own gestures to draw on. And so, in both workshops of the play to date, a whole new gestural language was developed that was based on universally recognized Elvis Presley and Fan gestures. Conversely, it did make sense to use the traditional Noh walk and to use the circular movement patterns of Noh dance because these conventions communicated to the audience right from the beginning that this was not going to be a realistic play, that the characters were otherworldly, and that time and space were being abstracted.

Dance: As mentioned before, the circular floor patterns used in Noh dances were employed for Judy's trip to Graceland, The Dance of Many Elvis's and The Dance of Loneliness. These, too, were adapted for an American audience. For example, none of the characters carried silk fans. Judy's trip to Graceland at the top of the play was accompanied, instead, by abstracted driving gestures made with her hands. "The Dance of Many Elvis's" and "The Dance of Loneliness" were accompanied by abstracted Elvis gestures, such as the wiggle, the leg shake, and numerous other Elvis poses and hand gestures. The Fan Dance [which refers not to silk fans, but to Elvis Fans] was accompanied by the hand and body gestures exhibited by women at his concerts.

Gestures: The gestural language developed for both workshops was perhaps the most astonishing feature of creating an Elvis Noh drama because of what we discovered during the process of creating it. Many hours were devoted to watching videos of Elvis concerts as well as newsreels of his Fans. We soon realized that there were certain "signature" Elvis poses and gestures, which have become iconic in our culture. They are known by everyone who sees them—even those people who never saw Elvis in concert and do not consider themselves fans. In this regard, they are like the weeping and sitting gestures of Noh, which were known to its audience. Moreover, when these gestures and poses were abstracted, and slowed down, they were quite elegant and beautiful to watch. They adapted easily to the graceful aesthetic of Noh. We also began to notice a similarity between these gestures and those found in religions around the world. It is well documented that Elvis got his "wiggle" from watching Southern Baptist preachers in the pulpit, but he also used other religious gestures that seemed to be more subliminal in nature. Elvis had a particular hand gesture that we dubbed "the benediction" which he would perform at the end of his concerts. It was identical to the blessing gesture made by a priest during mass. Likewise, the Fans had a hand gesture which was identical to the one made by worshippers of all religions where the palms are opened and raised to the heavens to let in the holy spirit. Fan behavior often exhibited the characteristics of trance dance found in Asian cultures, as well, and contained movements and gestures associated with religious ecstasy. Elvis's funeral bore a striking resemblance to the Ayatollah Khomeni's, with both the Faithful and the Fans throwing themselves on their coffins, and the streets of Tehran and the lawn of Graceland lined with people prostrate with grief. That the "Church of Elvis" was formed after his death and continues to have a strong following was no surprise to those of us who worked with this material and found ourselves dealing not so much with a rock 'n roll legend, but rather, a religious phenomenon.

Costumes and Masks: This is the other element in the play, besides the music, that takes a departure from the conventions of Noh. In addition to his vocal and gestural signatures, Elvis also had costume signatures—blue suede shoes, the famous gold lamé suit, and later, the white glittered pantsuit from his Las Vegas years (which admittedly resembles Kabuki more than Noh). Again, to dress the actors in traditional Noh gowns would be contrary to the spirit of Elvis, and so, his signature costumes were used instead. Elvis Fans, likewise, have a certain look to them: the women have "big hair," and adorn themselves with Elvis jewelry, pictures and iconography. The difficulty we encountered in costuming the Fans was to stylize their clothing and hairstyles without throwing the play into comedy or satire. Miguel Angel Huidore, who designed the costumes in the Lang workshop, found the perfect balance by retaining the recognizable Elvis Fan look but dressing them all in white, making them look like religious novitiates. It gave them grace, elegance and dignity. The Memphis Mafia were dressed in the traditional garb of body guards, complete with sunglasses and look-alike Elvis bouffants. And finally, masks were not used in either workshop. My nod to the mask convention of Noh is in the role of The Man [the first incarnation of Elvis], which must be played by a black man wearing a white Las Vegas pantsuit. Not only does having a black actor serve to mask the identity of Elvis, it is also my own small way of acknowledging the African-American community from whom Elvis took most of his music.

Directing my own work is not something I normally do as a playwright, but implementing these non-textual elements was a necessary step in the process of finishing the play and making *Blue Moon Over Memphis* work as a Noh drama. I have since gone back and added stage directions to the script to give the reader some indication of where these music, dance and gestural elements accompany the text, but the directions are minimal, and don't explain how these elements work. Hopefully these notes, combined the stage directions and a study of the Noh, will provide a little more guidance on what a contemporary Elvis Noh drama should look like when it is fully produced on the stage.

Deborah Brevoort

The
Raunchy Dame
in the Chinese
Raincoat

John Ford Noonan

John Ford Noonan

The plays of John Ford Noonan include *All She Cares About is The Yankees,* *Concerning the Effects of Trimethylchloride, A Coupla White Chicks Sitting Around Talking, Getting Through the Night, Good-By and Keep Cold, Heterosexual Temperature in West Hollywood, Lazarus Was A Lady, Linger, Listen To The Lions, Monday Night Varieties, Music From Down The Hill, My Daddy's Serious American Gift, A Noonan Night, Nothing But Bukowski, Older People, Pick Pack Pock Puck, Rainbows for Sale, Recent Developments in Southern Connecticut; Sneaky Bit To Raise The Blind; Some Men Need Help; Stay Away A Little Closer; Talking Things Over With Chekhov; Where Do We Go From Here?;* and *The Year Boston Won the Pennant.* He has also acted in the films *God Has A Rap Sheet* and *Flirting With Disaster.*

This Play Is Dedicated to Jesse Sage Noonan and Marj Mahle

characters (In order of appearance)

GINO KRAMER

HARRY CONSTANTINE

MARLA MAUER

time

Early October, early evening. The present.

place

West Hollywood, California, 733 North Kings Road, Apt. # 336C. It's messy and crazy. In one corner neatly arranged video equipment: TV, VCR, video camera. In other, pile of newspapers, old and yellowing. In 3rd corner, dog bowl and water. Center of room, couch, wide, white and wonderful. Pictures on wall: Howdy Doody next to Van Gogh, Mickey Mantle next to Matisse. Kitchen area, table with phone in it...

• • •

[*Lights up! Noise at door, lock opens and two men enter carrying a rolled up 8-foot rug. Appearing first is* GINO KRAMER, *dark, tall, early 40s. He wears thick glasses. He is carrying front end of rug. Appearing second and carrying back of rug is* HARRY CONSTANTINE, *tall, thin, blonde, earßly 30s. Rug is very heavy. As they enter, they are winded and tired...*]

HARRY Gently, gently.

GINO Where?

HARRY The couch!

GINO The floor.

[GINO *about to toss his end of rug to floor only* HARRY *bellows up.*]

HARRY I said, the couch!

GINO I just had it cleaned.

HARRY One, two, three and toss.

GINO But—

[HARRY *starts "One, two, three,"* GINO *joins in and they toss rug onto couch.* GINO *is the more exhausted. He coughs and wheezes.*]

GINO Heavy! Whew!!

[GINO *crosses to refrigerator, takes out bottle of juice, offers to* HARRY.]

Fruit Delight?

[HARRY *waves his hand "No," stares at rug.* GINO *chugs from bottle, returns to refrigerator, replaces bottle and crosses back to* HARRY.]

HARRY So!

GINO So?

HARRY Whataya think?

GINO What about?

HARRY Our Chinese raincoat.

GINO Where?

HARRY There!

[HARRY *suddenly slaps hand against rug laying on couch.*]

GINO That's a rug.

HARRY Nope.

GINO Says who?

HARRY The guy.

GINO What guy?

HARRY The guy who gave me a note with the 1200 dollars inside.

GINO What guy gave you a note with 1200 dollars inside?

HARRY Remember when you were back at the bar.

GINO I hate when you start like this.

HARRY Do you remember or don't you?

GINO Of course I remember!

HARRY Then what's wrong?

GINO Cause you always say "REMEMBER WHEN YOU WERE BACK AT THE BAR."

HARRY Gino, listen—

GINO Why not say "REMEMBER WHEN WE WERE BACK AT THE BAR." Make me feel like there's two of us. I don't like separate and distinct. At night I sleep alone. Daytime I want to be part of something. Did we go to the bar together?

HARRY Yup.

GINO Did we both order Bud on tap?

HARRY Absolutely.

GINO Are you my best friend?

HARRY We're getting there!

GINO Do anything I ask?

HARRY   Name it and we'll see!

GINO   Practice the plural. Fuck the singular.

HARRY   O.K., we're both back at the bar, we're both slurping BUD. We're both watching the T.V.

GINO   When all of a sudden—

HARRY   THE SUPREMES blare on the juke!

GINO   Diana Ross always makes me piss!

HARRY   So you've got to go to the men's room. O.K., you're pissing and Diana's singing when BAM! This guy bops up to me and hands me this note with 1200 folded inside this note.

GINO   That's not what you told me, Harry, when I came back from taking a piss.

HARRY   Gino, listen—

GINO   What you told me, Harry, when I came back from taking a piss was…

[*Quoting, imitating.*]

"GINO, THESE TWO BROADS WANT US TO WATCH THEIR RUG TILL THE MORNING. THEN AROUND TEN THEY'LL TREAT US TO BREAKFAST AT THEODORE'S, TAKE US TO A MOVIE, AND THEN COME BACK HERE AND HUFF AND PUFF US TO DEATH."

Harry, why'd you lie to Gino?

HARRY   Cause you were smiling.

GINO   Come again.

HARRY   When you came back from taking a piss, you had such a beautiful smile on your face, I just—

GINO   I smile all the time.

HARRY   No you don't.

GINO   I'm smiling right now.

HARRY   No you're not.

GINO   Bullshit. I'm beaming from cheek to cheek.

[HARRY *runs to bathroom and returns with a mirror.*]

HARRY   Look!

GINO   Oh, shit!!

HARRY   Now you know.

GINO   All along I thought I was—

HARRY   Exactly!

GINO   While in actuality what I really was—

HARRY   Precisely!

GINO   My face wasn't doing what I thought it was. My face was, in the strictest sense, not very much of a friend.

HARRY   I couldn't put it better myself.

GINO   Thanks for drawing attention to a very serious flaw in my already shaky make-up.

HARRY   Hey, Pal, anytime!

GINO   So where's the note?

HARRY I ate it.

GINO What did it say?

HARRY [*Quoting.*] "HERE'S 1200 TO WATCH MY CHINESE RAINCOAT. MEET YOU BACK HERE, 12 NOON."

GINO How did they sign it?

HARRY "A GENEROUS FRIEND IN DESPERATE TROUBLE."

GINO Was there a P.S.?

HARRY That's why I ate it.

GINO Say the P.S.

HARRY P.S. "NO MATTER WHAT, DON'T LET YOUR SCUM-BAG HALF-A-FAG JERK-OFF PUSS-BRAINED LITTLE DICK APE OF A FRIEND LOOK INSIDE MY CHINESE RAINCOAT."

[*Pause.*]

GINO They called me an ape, huh?

[*Suddenly GINO bursts into loud and full-bodied laughter.*]

Am I laughing?

HARRY Yes!

GINO I'm not laughing like before with the smiling?

HARRY No!

GINO Ape, huh? Shit! Fuck 'em!! What do they know?

HARRY To call you an ape they can't have the slightest idea of how—

GINO Do they know that during the war I personally saved more than—

HARRY Of course not!

GINO Or that the Yankees once offered me almost—

HARRY How could they?

GINO Or that I was offered a chance back in '69 to actually—

HARRY Not a chance!

GINO Or that... or that... or that...

[*Pause.*]

If they hadn't used forceps, I'd have been as handsome as you.

HARRY Fore-WHAT?

GINO Back when I was born, I had a huge head, disproportionately large, you know, inside my ma and when my ma tried to push me out, she... she, well, my head couldn't get through. They had to reach along the walls of my mother's, you know, the doctor with this two prong thing that...that you know down at THEODORE'S when you go to the salad bar, the thing they give you to pick up the lettuce with.

[HARRY *shakes his head "Yes."*]

Well that's a forceps. Anyway, this forceps squeezed against the sides of my head, right here on both sides

[*Pointing to both sides of temple.*]

and in that way they dragged me out. The only problem was they squeezed so hard they altered the shape of my head from...you know...to...you know. Also, I had bruises along both temples that took over a year to go away. My mother kept a scrapbook. There's lots of pictures with me and these scary purple marks along both sides.

[GINO *lets out a long and loose laugh.*]

In second grade I didn't have to pay attention much cause I could read so well. I was always doodling. Mostly I drew pictures of how I would've looked if it hadn't been for the forceps. Sister Mary Felicitas grabbed one of my doodlings one day and said, I loved her way of talking.

[*Imitates* SISTER MARY FELICITAS.]

MR. GINO KRAMER, NOW WHAT HAVE WE HERE?

[*Imitates eight-year-old self.*]

"SISTER, THAT'S HOW I WOULD'VE LOOKED IF IT HADN'T BEEN FOR THE FORCEPS." Sister held the picture up. I was blonde and blue-eyed and handsome. Everyone laughed. For weeks after my classmates mocked me and chided me and called me "APEFACE." Guess what I did?

HARRY Wore a mask?

GINO Drew more and more pictures of how I would've looked if it hadn't been for the forceps.

[*Both men laugh.*]

There was no stopping me then. There's no stopping me now. There's no stopping now. I never stop believing. Just under the skin covering my chest is this set of doors that if you could open them, know what you'd see: This church all full of light with three altars filled with all these brightly burning candles. My three altars of faith, hope, and dreams. There's something in me that's great, Harry, and one day it's all going to come pouring out!

[*Suddenly* GINO *lets out that laugh.*]

Know what's the best part of being ugly: when someone likes

you, you always know it's for something else!!

[*Now both men laugh and hug each other. Pause.* HARRY *suddenly reaches inside jacket pocket and hands envelope to* GINO.]

HARRY Here.

GINO What?

HARRY Inside.

[GINO *opens envelope. Removes money, counts it out.*]

GINO 1000 dollars.

HARRY I kept 200 for running around.

GINO But—

HARRY Gino, for almost two months you've been letting me stay here.

GINO Till you find your own place.

HARRY Which I will, which I will.

GINO But that's not what—

HARRY And you've fed me!

GINO Harry, listen—

HARRY Bought me clothes!

GINO Harry, please—

HARRY Taken me to movies, given me pocket money.

GINO Harry, shut up!!!

[GINO *covers* HARRY's *mouth so he can't talk. Pause. Lets go of* HARRY.]

The 1200 wasn't bullshit.

HARRY [*Taking out 200 dollars.*] My 200 plus your grand equals 1200. So?

GINO Someone actually came up to you and handed you 1200 dollars to watch a rug?

HARRY Of course!

GINO And you never asked a question?

HARRY No reason to!

GINO And tomorrow you'll be back in the bar at noon with the rug?

HARRY Why not?

GINO Harry, listen—

HARRY All my life people have been coming up to me and giving me things. Back when I was a little kid, I was twice as cute as now, like maybe 2-1/2, 3 years old and already, boy, could I see people's eyes light up when I walked by in my sailor suit or my little Lord Fauntleroy or even nude. Even by then I had a big bouncer. I was always running down my front porch steps nude and bouncing my bouncer all over the place. Old ladies and even lots of young ones would come over and ask my Mom if they could rent me for a coupla hours or half a day so they could walk up and down Germantown Avenue pretending pretty little me was theirs. They'd offer all that money and Mom'd smile, "Why not!" Or back years and years ago when sad old Herbert Talmadge dying of cancer asked me up to his room and said—

[*Quoting.*]

"HERE'S A HUNDRED. NOW TAKE OFF YOUR CLOTHES, PARADE AROUND, AND EVERY TIME YOU PASS MY BED, SAY 'HERBERT OLD BUDDY, I LOVE YOU. THE WORLD'S GOING TO BE A SMALLER PLACE

WHEN YOU'RE GONE.'" "Herbert," I said, "Why not!" Or
what about last week at THEODORE'S when that tired old
queen gave me this leather coat cause he said I looked—

GINO O.K., Harry, O.K.!

HARRY Or a few hours back when they came up to me and said
"HERE'S 1200 TILL TOMORROW AT NOON." And then—
know what: They waited till you went to take a piss cause…

GINO Cause I'm ugly!

HARRY Cause you're nothing but WHY, WHY, WHY. WHY'S a lie.
Life's about WHY NOT. See, they knew you would've freaked
over calling the rug a Chinese raincoat or…

GINO But, Harry, why call something what it isn't?

HARRY They knew you would've WHY'D the whole scam to death.
Man, you've got so much going: heart and love and caring and
respect and openness, I mean, you gave a jerk-off like me shelter
and food and pocket money.

GINO Want me to tell you why?

HARRY Man, you've got…got shit going in full gear that I'll maybe one
day have one tenth of. You'd be a perfect father! What a coach
you'd make! As an older brother, you're a dream come true.

GINO [*Suddenly grabbing* HARRY.]
Now listen…

HARRY You only got one problem: you grab at things. You don't pet
them.

[GINO *releases* HARRY.]

Pet life, Gino. Don't grab at it. If someone with a '78 Chevy says

"SO WHATAYA THINK OF MY NEW CADILLAC?" say "WHY NOT!"

GINO Why?

HARRY If someone rips out their dick and says "SO WHATAYA THINK OF MY VAGINA?" say "WHY NOT!"

GINO Why?

HARRY It is right in this house and you don't even know it!

GINO Where?

HARRY The bathroom!

GINO What's in there?

HARRY Bukowski!

GINO What about Bukowski?

HARRY You've got a stack of his books in there by the bowl!

GINO And every morning when I take a crap I read a chapter. I know Bukowski. I love Bukowski. I live for Bukowski. My grave stone's gonna read: "HE READ ALL OF BUKOWSKI SITTING ON THE JOHN."

HARRY But he never let Bukowski into his life!

GINO What did you say?

HARRY That's what's so lousy about you people who read all the time: You never let your reading into your lives.

GINO Hold it, Harry!

HARRY The more you read romance novels, the more you're afraid of chicks. Detective novels make you scared. Sci-fi makes you paranoid. I mean, if anybody on this earth is a WHY NOT guy it's Bukowski. He never asks questions. He says fuck to logic. He goes with the flow.

GINO But—

HARRY Everytime a different woman comes on to him in his splendid 1978 novel WOMEN, all he does is smile and go along. WHY NOT.

GINO But—

HARRY Lydia, Nicole, Mindy, does he ever say WHY?

GINO Wait a minute—

HARRY Or what about the women in the mesmerizing story THE MOST BEAUTIFUL WOMAN IN TOWN. All he does is ride it out, go along, flow, flow, flow!

GINO Hold it! I thought you didn't read?

HARRY What am I supposed to do when I'm taking a crap? Yes sir, the most WHY NOT guy in the world and all he does is make you more WHY.

GINO Now listen…

HARRY Shut up! Gino, know what's the worse thing about your always asking WHY: it keeps you from me.

GINO Keep me from you HOW?

HARRY Let me ask you a question.

GINO Well… why… not! Yeah, WHY NOT!!

HARRY What beyond WHY NOT made me take the 1200 and the Chinese raincoat?

GINO I really...

HARRY Cause the 1200 was a way for me to pay you back, show you that I appreciate the chance you've given me only you...only you...

GINO Only I was so into my...

HARRY Of course!

GINO That you couldn't...

HARRY Exactly!

GINO So that you ended up feeling...

HARRY How else?

[*Pause.*]

Give me the thousand.

GINO What?

[HARRY *offers hand authoritatively.* GINO *reaches into pocket and hands money back to* HARRY.]

HARRY We'll do the scene again. Can you act WHY NOT?

GINO I'll try.

HARRY [*Handing money back*] Here!

[GINO *opens money. Overreacts being surprised at* HARRY*'s generosity. Overreacts response as well.*]

GINO Fucking WHY NOT!

[HARRY *takes back money, hands it back to* GINO *several times and each time* GINO*'s answer is the same.*]

Fucking WHY NOT! Fucking WHY NOT!

HARRY Have you got it now?

GINO I think so.

HARRY Let's practice!

GINO WHY NOT.

HARRY Hey, Buddy, that some set of tits you got there.

GINO WHY NOT!

HARRY So, how's it feel to be the king of Saudia Arabia?

GINO WHY NOT.

HARRY All joking aside, how's it feel to be first man ever to hit three home runs in an All-Star game?

GINO WHY NOT.

HARRY God, you're beautiful.

GINO WHY NOT.

HARRY Why?

GINO WHY NOT.

HARRY You've got it.

GINO I've got it.

HARRY Repeat after me.

GINO Repeat after you.

HARRY WHY is to die. Life's about WHY NOT.

GINO WHY is to die. Life's about WHY NOT.

[*Several times* GINO *repeats* HARRY's *sentence.* GINO *gets more and more excited, jumps around, suddenly lifts* HARRY *into the air, hugging him, spinning round and round.*]

       I love WHY NOT. It makes me feel big and safe and…and…
I'm a WHY NOT guy with a WHY NOT buddy and we're the
WHY NOT twins, I mean, WHY NOT! Harry, if I can stay
away from always questioning and just…just…

HARRY Oh, God!

GINO What's wrong?
       [GINO *smiles broadly.* HARRY *picks up mirror and shows* GINO *his smile.*]

       Holy shit!!

HARRY I know.

GINO Look at how much I…

HARRY Of course!

GINO Where before I was so…

HARRY Certainly!

GINO I mean if you hadn't…

HARRY Don't mention it.

GINO When I smile, I smile!

       [*Showing smile.*]

       Look, when I feel it, my mouth goes right along.

       [*Over and over* GINO *practices his smile. With each attempt it grows bigger, fuller, and wider.*]

Harry?

HARRY Gino?

GINO Let's hurt the heart of someone bad and mean.

HARRY Why not?

[GINO *runs and gets pair of scissors. Returns to couch with them.*]

What are you doing?

GINO YOUR SCUMBAG HALF-A-FAG JERK-OFF PUSS-BRAINED LITTLE DICK APE OF A FRIEND'S having a look inside.

[*Starts to cut red ropes that hold rug in place.* HARRY *stops him.*]

HARRY Listen, suppose…

GINO Why not!!

HARRY I mean, people who…

GINO Why not!

HARRY For example, when…

GINO Why not.

HARRY Stop with the fucking "WHY NOT."

GINO If you talk the talk, you gotta walk the walk.

HARRY But…

GINO Repeat after me!

HARRY The guy who gave me the 1200…

GINO   Repeat after me!!!

HARRY   Repeat after you.

GINO   LET'S HURT THE HEART OF SOMEONE BAD AND
MEAN.

HARRY   "LET'S HURT THE HEART OF SOMEONE BAD AND
MEAN."

[*Several times* GINO *and* HARRY *repeat chant. Finally* GINO *cuts chords. Rug
a.k.a chinese raincoat opens and* GIRL *rolls out. She is blindfolded, gagged, and her
hands are tied. She is small, blonde, and beautiful. Her name is* MARLA MAUER.
She seems to be having trouble. GINO *removes gag and she gasps for air. Takes several deep breaths and finds normal rate of breathing. Next she shakes free of chord on
wrists. Starts to take off blindfold, stops, laughs.*]

MARLA   I don't have to see you guys. I can tell from the hum.

GINO   Listen, if you'd like to …

HARRY   God, what a bod!

[*They both start toward her. She, still blindfolded, steps to side.*]

MARLA   My Chinese raincoat was on so tight I couldn't make out the
words but I sure could hear your hum. It was, well, you guys kept
switching leads. First, the strong, deep hum of a father's advice,
then the shock of a son's wisdom. Back and forth, back and forth,
two hums being passed. It gave me no hope. Made me hold on. I
knew that I'd make it out here and you two'd be…

[MARLA *removes blindfold. Sees* HARRY *and* GINO. *Reacts like she
already knows them.*]

Oh, God! It's you two!!

GINO   Excuse me but we've never…

MARLA The Beauty and The Beast. You guys always eat breakfast between 10:10 and 10:35 over at THEODORE'S on Santa Monica. You, Beast, what's your real name?

GINO Gino Kramer. Him, he's Harry Constantine.

MARLA Gino, you always eat two eggs over easy with two strips of bacon, home fries and a well-toasted sesame bagel. You're kind, considerate, and nice! Harry, you eat waffles and sausage and three tall glasses of milk when you're hung over but most of the time you have scrambled, toast and lots of decaf coffee. You're rude, loud, and vicious!

HARRY Hold it! No broad popping out of no rug's gonna tell...

MARLA Chinese Raincoat!

GINO She's right, Harry. Chinese Raincoat.

MARLA Me and my girlfriend Becky, we always get there between 9:30 and 9:37. We sit over in the corner. We order the cheapest breakfast. We play with our toast, touch our eggs, giggle like little girls, but mostly we just watch. We just sit, watch, and wait. We wait for a pair of guys who can be the answer for a pair of gals like us. THEODORE'S is mostly gay pairs of guys so you guys not being gay stands out. Excuse me, Harry, but would it be O.K. if you got a chair and sat right about... there...

[Points to spot far side of room.]

with your back to me.

HARRY Hold it!

MARLA Your eyes scare me.

HARRY What about him!

MARLA   His smile warms me.

HARRY   He hasn't got a smile!

[GINO *lets out the biggest, brightest smile seen in L.A. in years.*]

GINO   Harry, you gave it to me!

HARRY   Now listen...

GINO   Harry, say WHY NOT.

[HARRY *throws a fit of anger. Pouts, stomps feet, lets out soundless scream.*]

GINO   You passed it to me and now I'm handing it back.

[HARRY *grabs chair and crosses to far side of room. Waits for further instruction.*]

MARLA   Right there's perfect.

GINO   How about me?

MARLA   Closer.

GINO   [*Moving closer.*]

I'm smiling

MARLA   I feel warm enough to go on.

GINO   Go, Baby, go.

MARLA   Mindy's not pretty and I'm almost perfect so you guys looked like the ideal match.

GINO   How come you never came over?

[MARLA *gestures to* HARRY. GINO *laughs.* HARRY *leaps up paranoid.*]

HARRY   I felt that. It was a signal. Something about me.

[GINO *gestures to* HARRY. HARRY *sits back down, his back still to the action.*]

MARLA   It all started five years ago at BARNEYS BEANERY. That's where I first heard him.

GINO   Who?

MARLA   He was whistling.

GINO   What tune?

MARLA   THE HIGH AND THE MIGHTY.

[GINO *bursts into a whistle of The High and the Mighty. He smiles proudly.*]

He was much better!

GINO   Now listen here…

MARLA   Would you mind sitting over by Harry?

GINO   Yes, I would.

MARLA   Gino, I like your firmness! Don't move!!

HARRY   Hold it! Why didn't you say WHY NOT?

[GINO *gestures for* HARRY *to turn back around. Once again* HARRY *turns his back to action.*]

MARLA   It was Monday Night Football. I was in my Washington Redskin sweatshirt with no sleeves, my tight little Redskin hot pants, and my soft little Redskin booties. I was doing all these cheers. I had bet my last 200 on the Skins. It was back when Riggins was great and Joe Theismann was just coming into his own. The Skins lose. I go to pieces. I bang my head against the bar. I hear THE HIGH AND THE MIGHTY. I run around the corner. He's sitting there.

GINO   This guy who whistles so much better than me.

MARLA I plop down in the booth across from him. God, what whistling. When I was a little girl, my mother had this ratshit recorder, reel to reel, there were no cassettes then,... anyway, when I was lonely or hurt or scared, she'd play it for me. It was THE HIGH AND THE MIGHTY. See, it was my daddy whistling. He'd recorded it the day before he took off for Hong Kong when I was 8 months old. So there I was in BARNEY'S with this whistling sounding exactly the same as on the recorder and WHAM he stops and hands me 200 dollars. I yell out "HOW'D YOU KNOW THAT'S WHAT I LOST?" Next he smiles and says "I'LL GIVE YOU ANY WISH IN THE WORLD." I say back, "LET MY REDSKINS WIN THE SUPER BOWL." He smiles, "WHY NOT." He gets up and says, "I'VE GOT TO BE GETTING BACK TO HONG KONG." I knew who it was. I was too scared to say "DADDY, IT'S ME, MARLA." So I said "WHEN, DEAR SIR, CAN I EXPECT TO SEE YOU AGAIN?" "MEET ME HERE THE MONDAY AFTER THE SUPER BOWL. 8 P.M. BE ON TIME."

[*MARLA laughs and laughs and laughs.*]

Well, the Skins won the Super Bowl. The next night I go to BARNEY'S ten minutes early. As soon I hit the door, I heard this whistling. I ran to his table. Sat down. He handed me a thousand. Before I could say "THANKS" or "WHY," he says, "WHY ARE YOU ALWAYS COVERING YOUR NOSE WHEN YOU COME INTO A JOINT?" "I HATE MY NOSE. I'D LIKE A PERFECT ONE JUST LIKE YOURS." He says, "WHY NOT!" He makes an appointment with a plastic surgeon, I have my perfect nose!

GINO Who pays?

MARLA Him, of course! I meet him a few months later. He says "ANY-THING ELSE I CAN DO FOR YOU?" "I'D LIKE MY

BREASTS A LITTLE MORE UP-AIMED AND FULL!"
Another call, I've got perfect breasts. This keeps happening.
Pretty soon he's got me looking pretty perfect. We keep meeting.
Every time it's BARNEY'S BEANERY. We don't say a lot. Eat
an omelet. Discuss the weather. Argue about Rock-n-Roll. I love
Bob Seger. He calls him "A NO TALENT FAGGOT." I love it,
meeting like this. It's steady, regular, certain. Suddenly it's early
September, a little over a month ago. We have another of our
great BARNEY'S BEANERY meetings. The place is packed.
Loud. We're like two birds in a soundproof cage. Just as it's time
to hit the road, he takes my hand and says, "I GOTTA MAKE
ONE MORE TRIP TO HONG KONG, AND THEN WE
GOTTA TALK ABOUT IT." I smile. He hands me some more
money to keep going. "THIS IS TOO MUCH, DADDY."
"NOTHING'S TOO MUCH FOR MY MARLA." Without
even wanting to, it's been said. For years and years I've carried six
words in my head that never got out. "I'M YOUR MARLA.
YOU'RE MY DADDY." Now our six words have gotten out—I
am the daughter.

[*Pause.*]

We hug good-bye. We make a date for a week ago last
Wednesday. "EIGHT P.M. BARNEY'S BEANERY. DON'T BE
LATE." Like always, I'm there ten minutes early. Eight o'clock.
Eight-thirty. Nine o'clock. Finally at 9:24, I'm almost too scared
to breathe, I hear someone whistling THE HIGH AND THE
MIGHTY. I look up, and there he stands: tall, handsome, and
with that smile that he can overcome anything. He's got a big
single rose. "DADDY, A SINGLE RED ROSE IS MY
FAVORITE THING IN THE WORLD." "WHY NOT?"
Daddy hands it to me. I see the rose, sniff, a tear begins. Then I
see the tape taped across the knuckle of the hand that just handed
me my red rose. "YOUR PINKY'S GONE, DADDY."

"THAT'S ONLY THE BEGINNING, KID, UNLESS WE COME UP WITH THE $88,000 BY A WEEK FROM FRIDAY MIDNIGHT, THEY'LL KILL ME."

HARRY   That's three hours from now.

GINO   That is right out of Bukowski. Go on Marla, explain the $88,000.

MARLA   I'll do my dad.

[*Imitating father.*]

"MARLA, I TOOK THE MONEY TO MAKE YOU PER-FECT. THEY'VE CAUGHT UP WITH US. THEY SAY THEY'LL KILL ME UNLESS YOU DO 22 CHINESE RAINCOATS BY A WEEK FROM FRIDAY." You guys are my 22nd Chinese raincoat. A few hours back, when they loaded me up, they handed me this bag with two of my Daddy's toes in it and said, "WE NEED FIVE THOUSAND CASH TO WIPE THE SLATE CLEAN."

[*Suddenly* HARRY *jumps up like a little kid that discovers a secret. Crosses from his chair. He several times circles* MARLA, *laughing wildly, pointing accusingly.*]

HARRY   Who says they're his?

GINO   [*Pointing to chair.*]

Harry, back, NOW!!

HARRY   Your dad's toes. Let's see them. Get out the bag. Present the evidence.

GINO   Hold it! You can't expect—

MARLA   He wants the toes, fine by me.

HARRY   [*Continuing to bounce around.*]

All that eye shit didn't fool me. It didn't work. My eyes went on double duty overtime and now it's Joe Friday, move over.

MARLA Gino, please lift my skirt.

HARRY Let me.

GINO Harry, my fingers are fine.

[*Gino crosses to* MARLA *and begins to lift her skirt.* MARLA *flinches.*]

MARLA Go slow, it's all sore.

[GINO *lifts skirt full-up, revealing Ziploc bag filled half with blood containing what looks like two detached toes attached to* MARLA's *hip.*]

MARLA They stapled them into my skin just before they rolled me up.

HARRY Hold it! How do we know they're his toes?

MARLA Un-zip me.

[GINO *very carefully unzips Ziploc bag.*]

Gentle, gentle.

[GINO *finishes unzipping.*]

Now take out the note floating in the blood.

[GINO *carefully reaches into Ziploc bag and withdraws note covered in blood.*]

Now read aloud.

GINO [*Reading aloud.*] "DEAR MARLA: I DON'T WANT TO DIE. DO WHATEVER THEY SAY. LOVE, DADDY."

MARLA Now put it back and zip me up.

[GINO *carefully replaces note in blood of Ziploc bag and zips it up.*]

MARLA *lets out a horrendous scream.*]

GINO What's wrong?

MARLA The smell of my Daddy's blood.

HARRY I don't smell anything.

MARLA Where's the bathroom?

[GINO *points towards the bathroom, as* MARLA, *on the verge of vomiting, runs into bathroom and slams the door.*]

HARRY Gino, you don't believe this broad, do ya'?

GINO Harry, do you?

[MARLA *screams again from bathroom.* MARLA *charges out of bathroom carrying copy of Charles Bukowski's novel* Ham on Rye.]

MARLA *Ham on Rye* saves my life again.

GINO You know Bukowski?

MARLA He's my favorite all-time. He's the first thing I read every morning.

[*Exit* MARLA *back into bathroom.* GINO *sits on couch and begins mumbling numbers to himself.*]

HARRY Gino, what are you doing?

GINO Remembering.

HARRY Remembering what?

GINO The combination.

HARRY What to?

GINO [*Says to himself.*] 48-22-16

[*Pause.*]

22-48-16

[*Pause.*]

16-22-48

[*Pause.*]

I'll start with 48. I'm sure it's 48.

[GINO *crosses to a huge picture of Charles Bukowski on up-stage center wall.* GINO *swings picture hanging on unseen hinges. Secret safe is revealed on wall.*]

HARRY WOW!!

GINO No idea it was there?

HARRY Nope.

GINO Never saw it before?

HARRY First time.

GINO You're lying.

HARRY Say's who?

GINO One night I couldn't sleep. I stood off to the side like this.

[GINO *with arm extended towards safe stands aside, allowing clear visibility to safe from any vantage point in room.*]

Over in the corner you on your futon pretend to be sleeping. I felt like your eyes spying. Tell me the truth.

HARRY I was lying.

GINO   Never lie to me again?

HARRY   May my dick shrink six inches. So what's in the safe?

GINO $22,583 in cash, $50,000 in savings bonds, $30,000 in travelers checks, plus another $50,000 in CDs.

HARRY   That's over a hundred and fifty grand.

GINO   Plus seven first edition Bukowski hardcovers worth another fifty grand.

HARRY   I don't believe you.

GINO   [*Speaking in numbers.*]

48-22-16

[*Tries safe, it doesn't work.*]

HARRY   Try 48-16-22

[*Enter MARLA with copy of* Ham on Rye.]

MARLA   What's going on?

GINO   Trying to get you your money.

MARLA   Have you got enough?

HARRY   In that safe is over two hundred grand.

MARLA   I'll pay you back. I swear. Every last penny. Name the vig. I'll pay any interest. I'll do 22 more Chinese raincoats. Anything to save my dad. His name is Rudy Mauer. I'm Marla, Marla Mauer.

[*Offering* GINO *her hand.* GINO *does not take it.*]

GINO   You're very good. Where did Harry find you?

HARRY   Please, Gino, the safe.

MARLA If we don't get it open in time—

HARRY I said, "Where did Harry find you?"

HARRY Gino, what's going on?

MARLA This is why I hate guys, big, overgrown, ugly, hunch-backed, acned guys who hold money, power—

[GINO *lifts up MARLA's skirt and rips the Ziploc plastic bag off her hip. GINO holds up back of plastic bag, it is Velcro.*]

GINO Velcro?

MARLA It felt like staples going in, I was tricked.

GINO Sit quietly or I will totally re-arrange you.

HARRY I told you, Gino. Warned you the bitch was a fraud and a fake. Say, "Thank You, Harry."

[HARRY *grabs plastic bag from* GINO, *opens Ziploc, takes out fake toes and eats them. Spits out remains.*]

Fuckin' pigs knuckles. If this bitch pulled on me what she just tried to pull on you, I'd—

GINO You can stop, Harry.

HARRY I think we should fuck her up real good. Try and intimidate me, why.

GINO Know when I first knew about you, Harry?

HARRY Knew what?

GINO You didn't say anything about the weight of the rug.

HARRY What are you talking about?

GINO   All the way down Melrose from the RAINCHECK and then all the way down Kings Road to here.

HARRY   You up front, me on the heavy end. I remember wondering, "Boy, is this rug heavy."

GINO   But you didn't say anything. Why, Harry?

HARRY   I don't know.

GINO   You always stop and check everything. You're slow, practical, suspicious, you're usually so WHY that your why not shit before almost made me not go along.

HARRY   Hold it.

GINO   Like in the morning, early at THEODORE'S, we order the breakfast special and you always make the waiter taste it first.

HARRY   These days with all the diseases running around, a real man's gotta be careful.

GINO   Why, Harry, why?

HARRY   Why what?

MARLA   He wants to know why we were going to rip him off. Mr. Gino, he put me up to it.

HARRY   [*Slapping* MARLA.]

You're not going to believe this little bitch, are ya'?

GINO   Yes.

HARRY   What?

GINO   That story about the father. It sounded pure Harry.

[*Suddenly* MARLA *and* HARRY *burst into laughter and hug.*]

HARRY [*to* MARLA] Didn't I tell you?

MARLA [*to* HARRY] Dad, you were right.

GINO What the hell are you two pulling now? What are you two pulling?

HARRY It's mostly me.

GINO What?

HARRY The story of the father, Marla here's my kid. I'm the daddy. My real name's not Harry Constantine, it's Rudy Mauer. Most of what she said really went down between us.

MARLA He ain't lying, Gino. He told me all about you. I came lookin' for him a couple weeks ago, asked around Hollywood for a guy looking like my dad. Someone said I could always find him having breakfast with his big, ugly guy over at THEODORE'S.

GINO Hold it, where you been living?

MARLA Chicago. I been studying acting at this school there. Called the Goodman. The Goodman School of Acting.

HARRY She's a real talent, Gino. Can't ya' tell?

MARLA Anyway, I show up at THEODORE'S, and me and Becky, just like I told you before, we sit across the room and watch you two guys eat.

GINO Hold it, how come Harry doesn't recognize you.

MARLA I'm in my Midwest bimbo punk disguise.

[MARLA *races to rug, puts on spiked punk wig.*]

GINO Holy shit, I remember you now, too.

MARLA Two days in a row at the cash register I asked you for menthol cigarettes. Remember…

[*Playing Midwest bimbo punk.*]

"Hey, asshole. Got any weeds with menthol?"

HARRY   Gino, she's gonna make it big out here, can you tell?

MARLA   Anyway, last week, two mornings in a row, Gino, you don't show up.

GINO   I was off seeing my aunt in Santa Rose.

MARLA   Seeing my daddy alone, I sashay over to his table, looking like I look to you right now, plopped down and purred, "Mister, are you as hung as you're cute."

HARRY   To which I answer, "Reach under the table, baby, and find out for yourself."

MARLA   Only I scream out, "Daddy, that's incest," and rip off my disguise,

[*Rips off disguise.*]

and turn into the real me.

HARRY   It was the happiest I've ever been.

MARLA   Only I immediately get on his case, "Daddy, what are you doing hanging out with an ugly, overgrown jerk-off?"

GINO   And Harry said?

MARLA   "Baby, he's my best friend." Then I scream out, "But the guy's so dumb!"

HARRY   To which I answer "Baby, betcha 500 bucks we can't pull one of our cons on him."

MARLA I write up the skit, right, we just pulled on you.

HARRY We memorize it.

MARLA Rehearse once.

HARRY I figure a way to hide her in the rug, and, well, here we are.

[GINO *sits in his chair and puts his face in his hands.*]

HARRY Gino, you crying?

GINO Almost.

MARLA What's so sad?

GINO I cry when I'm happy. Ugly people do that a lot… especially people they care about like Harry here go out of their way to prove they're more valuable than they appear. Marla, thanks for thinking I was worthwhile enough to bet against, write a whole sketch about, and uh… When would you like to move in?

MARLA But—

GINO If you're part of Harry, you're part of me.

HARRY Baby, didn't I tell you he was the greatest.

MARLA I can move in tomorrow. Tonight I'll have to sleep in what I got on.

GINO I got a beautiful blue bathrobe my aunt from Santa Rosa gave me last time she came to West Hollywood. Would it be okay if I hugged you both and lifted you in the air?

[GINO *hugs them both, lifting them both in the air.*]

Excuse me, but it's time I was getting ready.

MARLA Ready for what?

[*Exit* GINO *into bathroom. Clicks lock.*]

MARLA Daddy?

HARRY Baby?

MARLA I was really wrong about him. Your friend is one of the greatest guys I ever met in my whole life.

HARRY The guy's a miracle.

[*Re-enter* GINO *in a beautiful tuxedo—cumberbund, shoes, the works.*]

MARLA You almost look handsome.

GINO The first annual Bukowski Club Ball. There's twelve of us. We all love Bukowski. Read his stories and novels every day. We all have three things in common: we're ugly, drink too much, and have a desperate need to find compassionate answers. Tonight's a very special night—we're inducting our first two women into the club. Not as full members, but as morning readers. OH GOD!

HARRY What?

GINO Wouldn't it be something if he showed up?

MARLA Who?

GINO Bukowski. He's always showing up drunk. Wouldn't it be something if he showed up sober? Twelve times I've met him at gatherings at BAROQUE BOOKS, and eleven times he's shown up drunk. I look up to him and love his genius and live for his latest sentences, but when he's drunk he brags and boasts, and well, it's pretty sad. I guess he's angry because he's been so good for so long and famous only recently. The only time he was sober, we got on like velvet and diamonds—jugging, kissing, disagreeing. Know what I'm going to do if he shows up sober?

MARLA   Tell us.

GINO   Grab two chairs and put them by the middle aisle with all his paperbacks overhead. He'll feel comfortable with all his own words so close. Anyway, I'll sneak him away, and we'll be sitting across from each other, and I'll take a deep mysterious sigh, and then I'll hit him.

HARRY   What with?

GINO   Blow by blow with what went down here today. Know what he'll say when he hears what went down here today?

MARLA   Tell us.

GINO   "That sounds like one of my stories. Gino, do you mind if I steal it?" Only I'll say, "Yup."

MARLA   But why?

GINO   'Cause I been looking for something to write about all my life, and you guys are it.

[*Hugging both of them.*]

The minute I get back from the ball, I'm gonna start writing about you two. Guard the fort, and don't eat all the peanut butter.

[*Crosses to door, comes back and kisses* MARLA.]

Thanks for making an ugly guy feel handsome. We're a real family. Wow.

[*Exit* GINO. MARLA *crosses to door to make sure* GINO *has left.* MARLA *then rushes into* HARRY's *arms and starts kissing him passionately.*]

HARRY   God, you get me hot.

MARLA I want to chew you good.

HARRY First things first.

[*They stop kissing and pull apart.*]

MARLA Hey, daddy.

HARRY Hi, daughter.

MARLA We sure fooled him, didn't we?

HARRY He's smart, but he ain't smart enough for us.

MARLA Get the tools.

[HARRY *crosses to rug and pulls out toolbox.*]

HARRY Even got a mini-acetylene in case I can't crack the combination.

MARLA You think you can crack it?

HARRY 48-22-16. Let's find out.

[HARRY *and* MARLA *cross to wall safe.* MARLA *hands* HARRY *stethoscope, continues to hold end and puts it next to combination.* HARRY *puts other end to ears. Unnoticed by* HARRY *and* MARLA, GINO *re-enters through door. Stands quietly.*]

GINO It's 22-16-48.

[MARLA *and* GINO *turn startled.*]

How about a little Bukowski in the dark before I cut your throats.

[GINO *hits light switch. Entire stage goes dark.* GINO *quotes briefly from Bukowski through scuffling, screaming, and shouting. Lights blast on full. Center stage,* MARLA *and* HARRY *sit in chairs tied by ropes. Their mouths are neatly gagged by masking tape.* GINO *stands next to them with huge kitchen knife. He cuts both throats.*]

Gurgling sounds, blood spurting everywhere. GINO *crosses to kitchen area, washes off knife, and puts it in the kitchen drawer. Crosses back to couch, takes out a pad and pencil and writes. He quotes each word as he writes it.*]

GINO AFTER HE CUT THEIR THROATS, HE CLEANED THE KNIFE AND PUT IT BACK IN THE KITCHEN DRAWER.

[*Pause.*]

AFTER HE CUT THEIR THROATS, HE CLEANED THE KNIFE AND PUT IT BACK IN THE KITCHEN DRAWER.

[*Pause.*]

What a nice opening to my first story.

[GINO *continues to write,* MARLA *and* HARRY *continue to bleed.*]

• • •

The Death of Bliss

Jules Tasca

Jules Tasca

Through Indiana University of Pennsylvania, Jules Tasca has taught playwriting at Oxford University in England and he has performed with a Commedia dell'arte group in Central Italy. He is the author of 120 (16 full length, 104 one-act) published plays that have been produced in numerous theatres from the Mark Taper Forum to the Bucks County Playhouse, as well as abroad in England, Ireland, Austria, Germany, South Africa, Canada, and Australia. He scripted *The Hal Linden TV Special* His *Llorana* and *Maria* were produced on National Public Radio. Other one-act pieces were broadcast in Los Angeles and abroad in Germany. He was the national winner in New York's Performing Arts Repertory Theatre Playwriting contest for his libretto *The Amazing Einstein*, which toured the country and played at The Kennedy Center in Washington D.C. He has adapted the stories of Oscar Wilde, Guy de Maupassant, Mark Twain, Robert Louis Stevenson, and Saki, and has modernized Aristophanes' *Ecclesiazusae* (Women in Congress). He has published new versions of *Hamlet* and *Macbeth*. His libretto for C.S. Lewis' *The Lion, the Witch and The Wardrobe* had its world premiere in California and played in London and New York and toured nationwide. For his play *Theatre Trip*, he was the recipient of a Thespie Award for Best New Play and his *Old Goat Song* won a drama critic's award in Los Angeles. His play *The Spelling of Coynes* and *Deus-X* have been included in *The Best American Short Plays* anthology. His tragic piece *The Balkan Women* won the prestigious Barrymore Award for Best Play. His play *The Grand Christmas History of the Andy Landy Clan* was broadcast on 47 national public radio stations. Mr. Tasca received a grant from the Pennsylvania Council of the Arts to develop a new theatrical form, the Eurhythmy, a system of movement of language, music, and sound. His tragedy *Judah's Daughter* received the Dorothy Silver International Playwriting Award. He won first prize in the Bucks County Writers Club Screenwriting Contest. Most recently his *play Live Drawing: A Portrait of the Mona Lisa* was published by the Dramatic Publishing Company. He is a member of New York's Dramatists Guild.

characters

KHALID AKKA   A young Palestinian

SANA AKKA   KHALID's wife

time

Present

place

A small apartment in Jerusalem.

• • •

[*Lights come up on* KHALID AKKA, *a young Palestinian man.* KHALID *paces nervously and smokes intensely. He looks at his watch.*]

KHALID   [*To himself.*] Why isn't she home? Sana…Sana…where are you?

[*He looks at his watch. He paces some more.*]

Where could she have gone?

[KHALID *lifts a coat from a chair. There is a vest under the coat. The vest is packed with explosives and held together with duct tape. He puts on the vest and looks in the mirror. He is proud of what he sees.*]

KHALID   Praise the name of Khalid Akka! Yes…yes…God is great.

[*He removes the vest-bomb and replaces it on the chair. He steps back and regards it. He hears footsteps. Quickly, he covers the vest-bomb with his coat. His wife,* SANA, *a young Palestinian woman, enters. She wears a head scarf and carries a small knapsack.*]

KHALID   Sana, where have you been?!

SANA   What's the matter?

KHALID What's the matter? I am waiting for you.

SANA I had an errand to run.

KHALID Errand?

SANA Yes, an errand. So? Usually, you spend your lunch hour with the men drinking tea and smoking and going on and on about the Jews.

KHALID Going on and on about the Jews...

SANA Well, you do.

KHALID Is that how you see me, your husband? As some kind of kiosk attendant who fills his free time with empty talk, going on and on about the Jews?

SANA I didn't say...

KHALID You said on and on...on and on about the Jews...as though your husband is nothing but a tea shop talker.

SANA It's not just you. Khalid, I didn't mean just you.

KHALID You meant what then?

SANA It's all of us. Who talks of anything but them? That's our lives now. The Jews and what they do to us.

KHALID The Jews are our oppressors. The Jews are our occupiers. The Jews stole our land. The Jews give us pain. People...people talk about what pains them, Sana.

SANA I know.

KHALID So until the Jews are gone, there will be no other topic but the Jews! Understood?

[*A beat of silence.*]

SANA Khalid, I'm tired. I don't feel so good. I don't want to talk about the Jews right now.

KHALID Sana, you have to talk about them now.

SANA Right now? Why?

KHALID Because...because Jews are an infection in the land of Palestine. You fight an infection before it kills everyone.

SANA I've heard it all before. Why at this moment...Will you stop pacing back and forth.

KHALID Sana...

SANA What?

KHALID My brother...he...he...

SANA Your brother what?

KHALID He came to me at the kiosk today. Then we came here.

SANA You brother, Ibrahim, he was here today?

KHALID Yes and he...he...

SANA Khalid, what?

KHALID Sana, I am being honored.

SANA You are being...

KHALID Honored. Yes, I am.

SANA What're you talking about?

[A beat of silence. KHALID looks at her.]

Khalid, what honor?...Husband?

KHALID   He, Ibrahim, he dropped off the vest.

SANA   The vest…you mean…Khalid, you mean one of those vests that…

KHALID   Yes.

SANA   A bomb?

KHALID   Yes.

SANA   No…

[KHALID *crosses and removes the coat from the chair, revealing the vest-bomb.* SANA *slowly crosses to it.*]

KHALID   Don't touch it.

SANA   You…you know about these…these vests.

KHALID   They trained me and Ibrahim both. Showed us how to…how to detonate it.

SANA   When did you…

KHALID   We took training.

SANA   Secretly.

KHALID   Secretly. Yes. Sure. From the authority. Yes, I did. See there are two metal pieces here in the pocket covered with tape. Once you remove the tape from each strip of metal, you…you touch the strips together and…

SANA   And you are dead…you don't need much training to be dead.

KHALID   It is an honor to be selected.

SANA   I didn't…

KHALID You didn't what, Sana?

SANA Know. I didn't know that...

KHALID That I had placed the name of Khalid Akka on the list of those willing. No, you didn't know. I couldn't tell.

SANA Couldn't tell me? Couldn't tell your own wife that you took training.

KHALID I told no one. The handlers told us to tell *no one*. There are those among us who for Israeli money would turn us in.

SANA And Ibrahim, his name is on the list too?

KHALID Sure.

SANA Why then you?

KHALID The authority chooses...

SANA Why you and not Ibrahim?

KHALID I think...I think because...because I work the kiosk at the Grand Market, no one would suspect me. It'll be crowded tonight, because of the start of the Jewish holiday and I...

SANA And you're going back to work with this vest under your coat to...to...

KHALID My loving wife...I knew this would be hard for us.

SANA But your loving wife has nothing to say about it.

KHALID Why would a wife or mother or any woman have a right to keep me from...from...from meting out punishment to the infidels?

SANA No. How could any woman keep you from such an honor.

KHALID   It is an honor, a high honor.

SANA   Khalid, we stand in our apartment and we talk of your death as if you were going out for cigarettes.

KHALID   No. I…I am on edge. My palms are wet. My nerves are all out of their pockets. But…you…you are supposed to hold your head up high, my loving wife. There is…underneath the tension…there is a pride…

SANA   Pride.

KHALID   Don't you feel it?

SANA   I'm to be proud also?

KHALID   You're not? You're not proud?

SANA   I am just…just shocked…

KHALID   I know.

SANA   You took training…you're serious…

KHALID   I think we must battle the occupation. That fight is the marrow in these bones.

SANA   I just feel numb…numbness…

KHALID   My wife, you must understand. My brother told me—no promised me, vowed to me—that you would be taken care of. You will stay in the apartment. You will receive money regularly. You will be celebrated as the wife…

SANA   Who lost her husband.

KHALID   *As the wife of a martyr.* Thousands will march through the streets for my funeral. Our men will carry my coffin draped with the flag. The shots they fire in salute of me shall be my voice from the grave...and you...Sana...will march with me and wear my honor like a queen's crown.

SANA   Khalid...Khalid...how full the pride that overflows those eyes, eyes more precious to me than all the martyrs in heaven.

KHALID   Sana...

SANA   You can strike me if you will, but no, I will not lie to you. I do not respect this anymore.

KHALID   Wife...

SANA   For the Jews we are destroying ourselves. For the Jews we rupture our families. In my bones there is only sorrow.

KHALID   You dishonor your own brother by saying this. Your brother, Hanni, honored your family by...

SANA   Driving a car of explosives into a restaurant. Don't let me remember. My Hanni...

KHALID   He killed eight Jews and injured over twenty more.

SANA   And killed three Palestinians on the wait staff. Our hate bites its own tail.

KHALID   It's a war of sacrifice.

SANA   I know. I grew up without a brother.

KHALID   He was a warrior, the same as Ibrahim and I are. Oh, Sana, I know that life is bliss, but it is the bliss of a moment. After such a sacrifice is the bliss of forever. The bliss of God. Your brother, Hanni, is with Allah. He is a hero. I always wanted to live up to your brother's name.

SANA   When Hanni died it was the death of bliss for me. And now...now...husband, how can a wife be happy?

KHALID It is not a time to be happy. It is a time to be strong. I…I will miss you too. So much. But look, I go to God and His paradise.

SANA And so you do. You go to God and I, your wife, go to the funeral.

KHALID Sana…Sana, I…I never thought you'd have this attitude.

SANA How could you? How could I? We don't know the burn until the lightning hits.

KHALID We're at war. These are the acts of war. We're all soldiers, all of us, all of our people. I'm just waiting for you to say something that makes me know you understand…Wife? Sana? I…I thought…I mean to say, I saw this time as us holding each other as tight as love can grip two people and I thought…

SANA I don't feel that way. I'm sorry.

KHALID This stance you've taken…

SANA What stance?

KHALID This wall you're putting up. One could interpret this as being against the uprising.

SANA We live the uprising. We breathe the uprising. Today I'm breathing uprising instead of air. It's choking me that you…that you…

KHALID You would talk me out of it…

SANA I love you. In the eye of the uprising I love you.

KHALID I know you do. And I…I am…I am afraid, Sana. I am. But my…my duty to my country…

SANA What about your duty to the living. Your…your family…your…

KHALID My mother knows. I stopped there already. Oh, yes, she was upset, but Ibrahim and I soothed her with the pride that will come after...

SANA Pride. What are we to do with this pride. How can we love pride more than life?

[KHALID *crosses to the chair holding the vest.*]

KHALID I have no more time for women's hysterics. I am leaving. Say something to me, Sana. Say something to me that will last me forever...Sana?

SANA I am going to have a child.

[*A beat of silence. He crosses from the chair to* SANA.]

KHALID Are you saying this because...

SANA *I am going to have a child.*

KHALID Sweet heaven...oh, Sana...you are...

[*He embraces her.*]

SANA Yes...I was at the clinic this morning.

KHALID You were at...

SANA Yes, the clinic. That's why I was late.

KHALID And the doctor confirms that...

SANA Yes. Two months.

KHALID Pregnant...

SANA I am two months...

KHALID Two months along. Oh, my Sana...oh, my dear wife...

SANA I came home today to tell you of this honor.

[SANA *moves away from him.*]

SANA But now there is…there is an ache in my stomach. Today, when the doctor told me, in my womb I felt a beautiful sensation, a tingle of joy. Now…now, there is discomfort there…a gnawing, as if what's inside me recoils with a little startle of grief…

KHALID Now, after almost two years…now…now you become…

SANA If I…If I had known…Oh God if only I had known…

KHALID There was no way to know that I would be selected.

SANA No. No. I know that. But surely now you…you can…

KHALID I can what?

SANA You can…you can call Ibrahim. You can call your brother and you…

KHALID I can do what? Call it off? Back out?

SANA You must…

KHALID How? How can I call it off? The leadership. They're expecting the Grand Market of Jerusalem to be a windstorm of shrapnel. They expect Jewish flesh and oppressors' mouths to foam blood. They expect the air as thick as cream with their cries and moans …

SANA And what about your own flesh, husband?

KHALID It doesn't matter. I swore during training by Almighty God who holds the heavens above our heads, Sana, that the Jews will never live secure until they leave the land of Mohammed.

SANA And what about this child who sits here in the limbo of life and waits for the world to pull him out?

[*A beat of silence.* KHALID *stares at her. Then he crosses away.*]

KHALID   I...I...I never...I never counted on such a thing. You—my wife. I made Ibrahim promise to Allah that you would be taken care of. But I never counted on...on...

SANA   You know what it would be like, Khalid, for a child to call you father? Do you know how it will feel to have him or her run to the door when you come home? To have a bouquet of kisses flood your face? And there would be more pride in that than having your picture in your mother's front window dressed in carnations and draped with a flag dripping with honor.

KHALID   Oh, my Sana, how much I love you. Your words are still electric to me. Sana...Sana, love of my life, you are trying to change the world with your love of me.

SANA   I won't say I'm sorry if...if what I say changes your mind.

KHALID   But it's not so simple. Women. Wake up. Everything's so easy for women.

SANA   Only men say that.

KHALID   Sana, it's not possible for me to...

SANA   Why not? Call Ibrahim. Tell him what happened.

KHALID   Sweet woman...

SANA   Please...If you love me...please...

[SANA *crosses to the table and picks up a cell phone. She crosses back to* KHALID *with it. She hands it to him.*]

Please...

[KHALID *sits.*]

KHALID   I...I will be called a coward. Sana, the leadership doesn't care about your baby.

SANA   Our baby.

KHALID   That baby...my son...will be told of this if I back out. You know how a reputation gotten is a brand forever here. Khalid Akka, they'll say, he was chosen to sacrifice for his people, for Palestine, for our children's future and he...he...

SANA   We can go away.

KHALID   [*Rising.*]

They'd still all know. My family, my friends. My brother and mother disgraced. Wherever we went, we'd trail my wobbly reputation behind me.

SANA   I want my husband with me. If that makes me a traitor so be it.

KHALID   Don't say that. Ever...you are not a traitor. You are the wife of Khalid Akka. My son will never be disgraced by his father. I...I...I leave to you and him a legacy of honor...

[KHALID *embraces her. Then he crosses to the chair and puts on the vest, next his coat to mask the vest.* SANA *stares away.* KHALID *crosses back to her.*]

KHALID   SANA...I love you...Sana...But I must. It is impossible to do otherwise...God is great. He has seen fit to leave me alive in you...

[KHALID *kneels and kisses* SANA's *stomach.*]

God is great, Sana...Sana . . .

SANA   [*Softly.*] God...is...great...

[KHALID *rises and kisses her.*]

KHALID   Pray for me...

[KHALID *exits.*]

SANA

[*As lights fade.*]

I pray...I pray...I pray that—boy or girl—I pray that I lose it...I pray that I never have it...I...I pray...I pray...I pray...

. . .

Leash

Peter Maloney

CASSIE JESSUP   Julie Jesneck

Peter Maloney

The plays of Peter Maloney, *Lost and Found*, *Pastoral* and *Last Chance Texaco*, first produced at Ensemble Studio Theatre, are published by Samuel French, Inc. A recent play, *In the Devil's Bathtub*, was published in the *Kenyon Review*. His adaptation of Machiavelli's *Mandragola* was commissioned by Washington, D.C.'s Shakespeare Theatre and was produced there under his direction. Four autobiographical pieces, *Accident*, *My Father's Funeral*, *Accordion Dreams* and *Kolossal Hero* have been performed by the author at Ensemble Studio Theatre, and *Accident* was published by Faber and Faber in the anthology *Marathon 2000*. *Between the Acts* appeared in Broadway Play Publishing's anthology *Short Pieces from the New Dramatists*. A director and actor as well as a writer, Mr. Maloney directed Sandra Bullock in Larry Ketron's *No Time Flat*; Kevin Bacon in the American premiere of John Byrne's *The Slab Boys*; Tommy Lee Jones in Jack Gilhooley's *Time Trial*; Phyllis Newman and Adolph Green in Murray Schisgal's *The New Yorkers*; and Thomas Gibson and Lois Smith in Romulus Linney's *Juliet*. He starred with Estelle Parsons in David Hare's *The Bay at Nice*, and with Brooke Adams in *The Cherry Orchard*. He has been seen on Broadway in *Judgment at Nuremberg*, with Maximillian Schell; *Stanley*, with Antony Sher; Pavel Kohout's *Poor Murderer*, with Maria Schell; Eugene O'Neill's *Hughie*, with Ben Gazzara; and in the Lincoln Center Theatre productions *Dinner at Eight*, *Arcadia*, *Carousel*, *Six Degrees of Separation*, *Abe Lincoln in Illinois* and *Our Town*. He has appeared in 47 films, including *K-Pax*, *Boiler Room*, *Requiem for a Dream*, *The Crucible*, *Washington Square*, *JFK*, *Desperately Seeking Susan* and John Carpenter's *The Thing!* Mr. Maloney, a member of Ensemble Studio Theatre, the Actors Studio, and an alumnus of the New Dramatists, is a Fox Foundation Fellow.

characters

CASSIE JESSUP

place

Abu Ghraib prison, Iraq

time

October 2003

The Stranger is necessary, and antagonism directed against him
has a biological basis beyond wishful denial.

—Robert Ardrey, *The Social Contract*

They wanted to know why I did what I did
Well sir I guess there's just a meanness in this world.

—Bruce Springsteen, *Nebraska*

• • •

[*An open area between rows of cells in a prison in Iraq. Industrial lights hang from the ceiling, Electrical wires hang down. In a corner of the space, file boxes broken open, files spilling onto the floor. Old office furniture scattered about, a metal desk on which sits a computer monitor and keyboard. Swivel chairs, some upturned. Against the Stage Right wall, metal buckets full of water.*]

[*In the dark, sound of iron doors slamming shut. Echo of men shouting in Arabic, Sound of dogs barking. In very dim light, a figure, silhouetted, is pulled to center stage from up right by a strap stretching off down left at floor level.*]

CASSIE MOTHERFUCKER! Hey! Get back here, you!

[*SLAM. Lights up on CASSIE JESSUP, holding onto what we now realize is a long leather leash. In her other hand she holds a baseball. She jerks the leash, the pulling stops. She looks at us.*]

'Scuse my French.

[CASSIE *is in her twenties. Southern. Cute, in a kind of dirty way. Sweating. Hair cut short, like a boy's. She wears U.S. Army fatigue pants in a camouflage pattern and an olive-drab tee-shirt. Combat boots.* CASSIE *smiles, freezes, and there is a bright flash, as if someone has just taken her picture.*]

First thing is, you gotta show 'em who's boss. With a dog like this one…An' he's a big dog…Aren't you?

[*She jerks on the leash.*]

Yes you are, you're my big boy. With a dog big as this one, see, you got to let him know you're in control. At all times. He may be bigger'n me, but he knows who's in charge. Don't you boy? Hey, hey, HEY!

[*The leash tightens and she is pulled off balance. With both hands she pulls the leash until she is once again at Center.*]

That's why it's important you got the right leash. Thisn's nylon web. Tie-down strap I found up on Tier 2. Leather makes a good leash. It's got some give to it. Canvas is good. You can throw canvas in the washer when it gets all slobbery and disgustin'. Some folks like a chain, but a chain is heavy. Big dog, pullin' you this way an' that, you gotta ask do you want to add to the weight by using a heavy chain as a leash? Then there's your collar. Before you choose your collar, you gotta think about what you're tryin' to do. The purpose of the collar is to what? To *guide* your dog. And when you got to, to *check* your dog.

[*She jerks on the leash.*]

Like that. That's called abstention training. Make your dog stop doin' somethin' *he* wants to do but you don't want him to. That's called negative reinforcement. Like a bitch snaps at her nursin' pup, he bites down on her teat too hard.

[*She jerks on the leash.*]

That's a check. Hey, fetch!

[*She tosses the baseball offstage, waits.*]

You don't wanta fetch? I had this dog one time? Clyde? He was a mutt. All my dogs're mutts, pure-breds're too high-strung. Clyde only had three legs. He was cool, though. Only thing is, he didn't like blacks.

I had this one friend, Jewel? Well, Jewel couldn't come into my yard at all without Clyde goin' ballistic. Barkin', snarlin', just about pullin' the back porch off the house. We kept him chained to that wrought-iron trellis deal Tommy made for Mama. 'Course Mama wouldn't let Jewel come in the house. An' Daddy didn't want me goin' to Jewel's house. So I didn't see too much of Jewel. Hey, what're you doin'? Fucker!

[*She takes a flat, leather slipper from her back pocket, exits Down Left. Sound of leather slapping. CASSIE returns, still holding the end of the leash and the slipper. She puts the slipper in her back pocket.*]

Gotta nip that kind of behavior right in the bud. Lot of folks say you gotta be *friends* with your dog, punishment'll backfire on you. But I've had lots of dogs and in my experience it don't hurt for him to be a little bit afraid of you. I mean, come on, who's the boss, you or him? Huh? Listen, *discipline* is not *cruelty*. That's my opinion.

There's a place and a time for everything. Isn't there, Abdul? And this is not the place for you to do your business. Place stinks to high heaven already from all you dogs. What the heck would it be like if we let you make a mess wherever you wanted? Right? That's right!

See, animals respond to *routine*, and one of the first things you gotta do is let your dog know where's the right place and where's the wrong place for him to do his business.

An' we take you to the latrine, and what do you do? You refuse to go. An' then what? We take you back to your crate and you make a mess and then we have to clean it up and we get upset, don't we? Or we don't clean it up, and *you* get upset. Either way, one of us gets upset, and we don't want that, now do we?

[*The leash has gone limp. She turns to shout over her shoulder.*]

Orin! He's smoked! He's tuckered out! And so am I! I think he's gone asleep! Or else he's dead.

[*She crosses down to look offstage left.*]

Not dead. Malingering. Take a break, Kasim.

[*She drops the leash, looks at us.*]

This wasn't my idea. Orin! Fuckin' pantywaist. Addicted to that air conditioner. I told him, you're gonna get sick you go back and forth between the hot and cold all day. Orin's from Pennsylvania. What's he know from hot? Says they got hot summers. Humph. Hot summers. Where I come from hot means you can't hang on the monkey bars without your gettin' burned to blisters. Streets in summer, you don't want to wear shoes with nails in the soles, 'less you want to feel like Jesus must've, walkin' that last mile. Hot ain't nothin' new to me.

Doesn't mean I want to be here.

Fuckin' shithole. You like it here, Mufasa? Course you do, there's no place like home, is there? No, sir. Yes, Sir. Sir?! What do I do with this haji now? He's done his laps! Orin! Corporal?

He's prob'ly chattin' up Remarque. You know Specialist Remarque, Kasim? Sure you do. You had her panties on your head the other night.

[*She takes camera from pants pocket, aims it off left, snaps a picture. FLASH.*]

Never thought you'd end up a screen-saver, did you?

[*She puts camera back in her pocket.*]

He better not be doin' nothin' more'n talkin' to her! Fuckin' dog! I know he's a dog. But what can I do? He captured my heart, Abdul....You know what? I'm gonna e-mail that fucker right now.

[*She rights a swivel chair, sits in it, scoots over to the computer on the desk, begins to type.*]

"Dear...Corporal...Roper. You...dog. Get...your big... wet...red...nose...

[*She turns to look off left, grins.*]

Thought I was gonna say somethin' else, didn't you?

[*She turns back to the computer.*]

out...of...that...bitch's...crotch...right...now. Or I'll have you fixed! Arf-arf. Your ever-lovin' Cassie Jessup, PFC." Ha.

[*She turns to look off left.*]

It's not fair, Abdul. This ain't even my job. I'm not MI. I'm not even MP. I'm just hangin' here with Orin. I'm only here at all because of him. He is my heart. My sweet...heart. My only love. He fills me up like no one ever did in this whole world...And he's good-looking, isn't he? That smile? Oh, he knows how to have a good time. Our last night in Virginia Beach? Just after we got our orders? *Shit.* I could tell you stories.

Good God in heaven, now what am I gonna do?

[*Cassie turns front. She suddenly looks stricken. To herself:*]

Fuck!

[*She covers her eyes with one hand, cries. Recovers. Wipes her eyes.*]

Asante sana

squashed banana

We nugu

Mi mi apana...

[*Quietly muttering Rafiki's chant from The Lion King, she crosses to the line of buckets against the wall.*]

Where's ol' Rafiki when I need him?

[*She lifts a bucket full of water, goes to Stage Left portal.*]

Time for your shower.

[*She empties the bucket of water on the creature just offstage. Then tosses bucket off left. She regards her soaked captive for a moment, then goes to the remaining full bucket, lifts it, pours it over herself.*]

Yeah.

[*She sets the empty bucket down as she shouts:*]

Hey, Remarque! Get down here, you cunt!

[*She starts doing kung-fu moves in slow motion.*]

We'll have it out, right here, right now! Wet Tee-shirt contest on A-1!

[*Her hands go to her breasts.*]

I'd lose.

[*She is at the computer.*]

Should I send this? Abed? Hell, why not? SEND. "Your mail has been sent."

He's good at what he does, the Corporal. He does this same thing in real life, you know. Corrections officer. Upstate New York. Lordin' it over shitheads like you. I don't mean rag-heads, sand-niggers. I mean American niggers. We call 'em blacks.

[*She rights another swivel chair, sits in it. During the following, she may spin around in the chair, scoot around the room kicking her feet against the floor. Cassie is deadly serious, but there is often something playful in her manner, even when she is talking about the most horrendous things.*]

It's all your fault, you fuckin' hajis. Everything was goin' good and then you had to go and do that. How could you do that? *Three thousand innocent people.* Motherfuckers. I got a question: What the *fuck* is wrong with you people? Huh? Do you think you are *ever* going to win? Do you really believe you are going to whip us? *Us?*

Let me tell you somethin, Said. There's a creek behind my house
back home. You know? Creek? Stream? Water? Like a *river*, only
smaller? Anyway, it's a beautiful creek when it's runnin'. Lots of
sunfish. Little fish? Taste great you pan-fry 'em. An' crabs.
They're really crayfish but we call 'em crabs. In the summer the
creek dries up, an' you can jump from rock to rock and catch 'em
in the shallows. Crabs are the fastest creatures. Little suckers
scoot back under the rock they see you comin', so you gotta get
behind the rock and then reach around and under slow then *quick*
snatch 'em up, toss 'em in the can. Well, we were down there
crabbin' this one day, an' Clyde was with us. Ol' Clyde liked
nothin' better'n the creek, and he's goin' nuts, jumpin' on the
rocks, fallin' in, shakin' himself off, barkin' the whole time. And
all of a sudden, Clyde is barkin' like he's hurt. I look, an' he's in
this one pool that's deeper than the others, we call it the clay pit.
An' he's tryin' to climb out, but he's slippin on the clay an' then
he's goin' under, An' I realize that somethin' is pullin' him under
an' then I know: the snapper's got him. Big ol' snappin' turtle,
you can go years without seeing him, but he's somewhere in that
creek, you know that, but you forget it, you know how you do.
So I call out to Walter the snapper's got Clyde, and he comes
runnin' from a little ways upstream. He's been smashin' beer bot-
tles against the lower dam there, but he comes runnin' when he
hears me call.

Walter's amazing. He's dead now, but...He was totally not afraid.
Of anything. He didn't jump in. He knew he did he'd never find
a purchase in that clay. What he did was, he just leaned over that
muddy pool and grabbed Clyde by the forelegs up near his
shoulders. Clyde was a big dog, but Walter pulled him right up
out of that water, with the snapper still attached, his jaws on
Clyde's lower right leg, just below the hock. An' Clyde is howlin',
(he bit Walter twice, we found out later), tryin' to get away from
whatever's got him by the leg.

You ever see a snapper? Ugliest reptile ever invented. Prehistoric fuckin' monster. You think those IRF dogs are scary? We put a snapper in your box with you and you'll turn state's evidence in a *big* hurry, believe me. You couldn't tell 'em enough *fast* enough. But *Walter*, like he's in some science fiction movie, Walter grabs the snapper around the neck *with his bare hands* and just starts throttlin' him. The turtle's eyes are rollin' back in his horny head, tryin' to get a look at what's got *him* now. For a minute or two, it's a stand-off, the snapper won't let go of Clyde, and Walter won't let go of the snapper. Clyde is howlin' and Walter's moanin' nngggg…nnnggg…nnnggg, an' I'm…I don't know, I was prob'ly cryin' about my poor dog, an' suddenly the turtle opens his jaws to try to get at Walter, not realizin' by doin' that he's lettin' loose of Clyde. An' then I'm holdin' the dog and Walter's draggin' the snapper by the neck upstream to the dam. There's all these rusty wires and rods stickin' outa the concrete and he wraps this piece of wire around the snapper's neck and hangs him up there on the dam. When we get back from takin' Clyde to the vet's, the turtle's still alive, scratchin' at the concrete, tryin' to push off from the dam with his flippers. But he wasn't goin' no place. Me an' Walter took turns throwin' rocks at the bastard. Hittin' him with sticks. Broke his shell all to shit. Took three days for him to die. We left him hangin' there, stinkin' in the sun. Flies had a field day. Clyde lost his leg. But he lived a good long time with just the three. He was a good ol' dog.

What's my point here? Do I have a point? I don't know.

Maybe it's…Maybe it's that Snappers are strong…an' nasty…an' tough. But they're dumb. An' they're not as strong as Walter.

[CASSIE *puts her hand on her belly.*]

I don't feel so good.

[She mumbles Rafiki's chant to herself.]

Asante sana Squash banana…Orin!…Come get this guy! He's softened up.

[CASSIE suddenly moves to the bucket she emptied over herself, drops to her knees and vomits into it. Her back to us, we see her muscles contracting, relaxing, contracting, hear wrenching sounds as she pukes hard into the metal pail. Finally, the retching stops and she rests, her head still in the bucket. Quiet moans. She lifts her head, turns front, wiping her mouth with her forearm. Wet dripping from her mouth, eyes and nose. Wasted, she sits on the swivel chair, leans forward, her head in her hands. After a moment, she raises her head, looks off Left.]

I got a question.

[She takes a folded, laminated card from her pocket, unfolds it, finds the phrase she's looking for, reads.]

Fee 'indi suaal.

[There is no response.]

[She looks up and off Left, then looks down at the card, looks for a phrase, finds it, looks up again.]

Aeish ismak.

[There is no response.]

What is your name?

[There is no response. CASSIE folds the card, puts it in her pocket, turns front.]

I didn't come here of my own accord. And I can't leave that way.

[*She takes the camera from her pocket.*]

Whoever brought me here will have to take me home.

[*She lifts the camera, aims it at us.*]

Inshaalah.

[*She takes our picture. FLASH.*]

[*Lights fade.*]

• • •

The Right to Remain

Melanie Marnich

Melanie Marnich

The plays of Melanie Marnich include *Quake, Blur, Tallgrass Gothic, Beautiful Again, The Sparrow Project, These Shining Lives* and *Cradle of Man*. *Cradle of Man* was developed at the 2005 O'Neill Theatre Conference, received its world premiere at Florida Stage in 2006, premiered in New York at the Women's Project the same year, and was a finalist for the 2005 Susan Smith Blackburn. *The Sparrow Project* was produced as part of Steppenwolf Theatre's First Look Festival in 2005. *Blur* received its world premiere Off Broadway at Manhattan Theatre Club and also won the Francesca Primus Prize from Denver Center Theatre. Two of her plays, *Quake* and *Tallgrass Gothic*, have premiered at the Actors Theatre of Louisville's Humana Festival of New American Plays. Her awards include two McKnight Advancement Grants and two Jerome Fellowships from The Playwrights' Center, the Samuel Goldwyn Award, an Ohio Arts Council Grant and the Selma Melvoin award from Northlight Theatre. Her plays have been produced or developed at New York's Public Theater, London's Royal Court Theatre, the Guthrie Theater, Arena Stage, Dallas Theater Center, Portland Center Stage, Geva Theatre, Hyde Park Theatre, American Theatre Company, HERE and Denver Center for the Arts. She has also received commissions from the Guthrie Theater, La Jolla Playhouse, Children's Theatre of Cincinnati, Children's Theatre Company of Minneapolis and Mixed Blood Theatre. She is a Core Member of The Playwrights' Center and a member of New Dramatists.

The Fifth Amendment reads: "Nor shall any person...be compelled in any criminal case to be a witness against himself." That is, we have the right to avoid self-incrimination. That is, we have the right to remain silent.

The Right to Remain was commissioned by Mixed Blood Theatre (Jack Reuler, Artistic Director), as one of ten plays for its Bill of (W)Rights project, a project designed to explore the state of the Constitution's Bill of Rights at the beginning of 2004.

167

characters

AMY   Late 30s.

PETER   Late 30s.

JOSH   Mid-teens.

place

Their kitchen.

time

The present.

· · ·

[AMY *and* JOSH *in the kitchen. Amy is putting dinner on the table. Josh clicks away on a computer in the corner. He never looks away from the screen. Not when he speaks, not when he's spoken to, not until later.*]

AMY   [*As she puts dinner on the table.*] You okay?

JOSH   Yeah.

AMY   You sure?

JOSH   Yeah.

AMY   You're sure you're sure?

JOSH   Yeah.

AMY   Good.

[*Beat.*]

JOSH   What's for dinner?

AMY   Chicken.

[JOSH *just grunts.*]

AMY With rice.

[*Just a grunt.*]

AMY And asparagus.

JOSH Folic acid. Cool.

[*Beat.*]

JOSH Mom?

AMY Hm?

JOSH You okay?

AMY Yeah.

JOSH Cool.

[PETER *enters, just as he ends a call on his cell phone.*]

PETER [*On the phone.*] No. No. No. No. No. No. No. Okay. Bye.

[*He snaps his phone shut.*]

I hate my job.

AMY You have to go back in?

PETER It can wait till morning.

AMY That's news.

[*He puts the cell phone on the table and kisses* AMY *nicely, a little flirtatiously.*]

PETER Look at you.

AMY What?

PETER You're kind of dressed...*up*.

AMY A little.

PETER You look really...hot.

AMY Stop.

PETER You do.

JOSH I am in the room.

PETER Then maybe you should leave.

JOSH Mom?

AMY Stay.

PETER What's the occasion?

AMY Nothing.

PETER Not me being home before midnight?

AMY I had a meeting.

PETER With who?

AMY Some guy I might be working with.

PETER Do I know him?

AMY Doubt it.

PETER Should I be jealous?

> [JOSH *snorts but never looks at* PETER.]

PETER Shut up. Your mom's gorgeous. And I'm not an idiot.

JOSH Smell the irony.

PETER   What's that supposed to mean?

[JOSH *shrugs.*]

PETER   Is there any way to slap the teenager out of him?

[*Dinner's on the table.* AMY *and* PETER *sit down.*]

PETER   Josh.

[JOSH *totally ignores him.*]

PETER   Dinner.

[JOSH *ignores him.*]

PETER   Come on.

[JOSH *ignores him.*]

PETER   Now.

JOSH   Mom?

AMY   [*To* JOSH.] It's okay, hon.

PETER   No, it's not. Get over here. Now.

[JOSH *ignores him.*]

PETER   What is it about "now" that you don't understand?

JOSH   Mom?

AMY   I'll warm your food up later.

JOSH   Cool.

PETER   No. Not cool. I mean it.

JOSH   Mom?

AMY   He's working on something.

PETER   Well he can work on it later.

AMY   No he can't.

[PETER*'s* *starting to sense that something's up. A weird connection between* AMY *and* JOSH *that doesn't include him.*]

AMY   [*Starting to eat.*] How was your day?

PETER   [*Trying to switch gears.*] Uh, fine.

[PETER *starts eating.*]

AMY   Good.

PETER   Busy. Crazy.

AMY   You like that, though. Salt, please.

[*He passes it.*]

PETER   Yeah. I guess.

AMY   That big account?

PETER   Yeah.

AMY   Who'd've thought snowmobiles could suck up so much time.

PETER   Hey, it's Minnesota.

[*To* JOSH.]

You've got five seconds.

JOSH   Mom?

AMY   [*Sharply, to* PETER.] Leave him alone.

[*Now* PETER *knows something's up.* AMY*'s too benign.* JOSH *is too focused on the* *computer. It's a tense, bizarre, forced normalcy. A strange current in the room. He tries to feel his way around it.*]

PETER You?

AMY What?

PETER Your day. How was it. Including the part about that guy that I don't like the sound of.

[JOSH *snorts.*]

PETER Do you know how bad I wanna hit him right now?

AMY My day was fine, thanks.

PETER You had a huge deadline or something, right?

AMY Missed it. Does this have too much salt?

PETER What do you mean you missed it?

[*As a command.*]

Josh.

[JOSH *ignores him.*]

AMY I mean five o'clock came and went and I turned in jack shit.

PETER You never miss a deadline. And you never swear.

AMY There's a first time for everything. Go fuck a duck.

PETER Amy?!

AMY [*Looking directly at him.*] Peter?

[*She looks at him until he squirms. For an instant, he's a bunny in the headlights. Then she looks back at her food.*]

PETER [*Trying to catch his breath after that weird moment.*]
So you, like, completely missed it?

AMY [*Eating.*] Mm.

PETER Well, that can't be good.

AMY Pretty bad, actually. The asparagus is limp. Think I'd get it right by now.

PETER Like "bad" as in "you might get fired" bad?

[*No answer.*]

[JOSH *is focused on the computer.* AMY's *focused on her dinner. The atmosphere is just too weird for* PETER.]

PETER [*Snapping.*] Get off that stupid computer before I throw it out the window. I hate that thing. It's sucking the testosterone out of you. Turn it off. Eat. Then we'll go play football or something.

JOSH We don't own a football.

AMY [*Focused on her food.*] Are you online?

JOSH [*Focused on the computer.*] I can be. Want me to?

AMY Go ahead.

JOSH 'Kay.

PETER You two are starting to freak me out.

[*To* JOSH.] Come. Here.

AMY Stay there.

PETER Come here.

AMY Stay.

PETER Come.

AMY Stay.

PETER Come.

[*Nothing.* JOSH *keeps typing like nothing's happening. Amy keeps eating. Nothing, except for* PETER'*s confusion.*]

AMY Did you remember bread?

PETER What?

AMY Bread. I asked you to pick some up.

PETER No. I forgot. I'm sorry. I was really distracted this morning when you asked.

I'm sorry.

AMY I asked yesterday.

[*That throws* PETER *for a loop.*]

JOSH Mom?

AMY Hm?

JOSH I'm online.

PETER Get off.

AMY Stay on.

PETER Off!

AMY On.

PETER [*Finally losing it.*] Off! You—

[*To* AMY, *who's about to say something.*]

stop. And you—

[*To* JOSH.]

get over here.

[*They don't react. They don't even blink. It's like they didn't hear him. Whatever the game is, it's becoming clear that* AMY *and* JOSH *hold all the cards.*]

PETER Are you people insane? You're like a couple of zombies! Who are you? Are you on drugs? What planet are you from? What planet am I on? You were normal this morning. Somebody spill their milk. Somebody burp. Somebody talk about their day and look at me while you're doing it.

[*Silence.*]

PETER You're giving me the creeps.

[*Finally,* AMY *looks at him point blank.*]

AMY Three.

PETER What?

AMY I said "three."

PETER Three?

AMY Two.

PETER Two what?

AMY Five. Four.

PETER What?

AMY Two.

PETER Your lottery numbers?

AMY Nine.

PETER *My* lottery numbers?

AMY No.

PETER A secret code I need to get into the tree house? Because that I'd believe right about now.

[AMY *just looks at him.*]

PETER Are you okay?

AMY They're hers, right?

PETER Whose what?

AMY The numbers in her phone number.

PETER The numbers in whose phone number?

AMY Three-two-five, four-two-nine—What comes after nine? What's the last number of her number?

PETER Amy—

AMY Couldn't you come up with a better excuse than "snowmobiles?"

PETER You mean my *job*?

AMY Snowmobile photo shoot, snowmobile trade show, snowmobile convention…

PETER This isn't even worth talking about. It's stupid. It's just…*wrong.* Five minutes ago I was jealous of some guy you dressed up for.

AMY My lawyer.

PETER What?

[*Beat.*]

PETER You're crazy.

JOSH You're busted, dad.

PETER [*To* JOSH.] Shut up.

   [*To* AMY.]

   You…are…so…wrong.

AMY Really?

PETER You think just because I'm working all the time?

AMY No. Because you say you're working all the time.

PETER You know I am. I call you from the office. You call me there.

AMY Cell phones changed the rules. Accessibility doesn't preclude guilt. As a matter of fact, it's the perfect cover.

PETER What?

AMY I got that from the lawyer. Pretty good, isn't it?

JOSH [*Still not looking away from the computer.*] Tell me the last number, dad. Of her phone number.

PETER There *isn't* one.

JOSH Yeah there is. And I already know it. Because I called the phone company and got your cell phone records. But I want you to say it. Say it and I'll stop. Two? Seven? Five? One? Nine?

PETER [*To* AMY.] God, what kind of bullshit is this?

JOSH If you don't say it, I'll type it in. It'll tell me her name and address. Then I can run a search on her. Credit. Credit cards. Parking tickets. Like that. I can find out where she went to high school. Which means, like, we find out how young she is.

If you say the last number, I'll stop. If you admit it. I'll turn off the computer and eat my vegetables at the table next to you. But if you don't, I'll put in the number. I'll find out where you took her for dinner. I can find out days and times. I can find what you bought her. I can find where you stayed. Where you fucked her. How much you paid for the room. Come on. What's the number? Just the last one. Then we can stop. If you admit it.

[*Nothing.*]

PETER Why is he...?

AMY The thing is, I had no idea. He's the one who figured it out. Not me. Not even close. I believed every late night. Every Saturday afternoon. I was thinking "Sure. Why not? Snowmobiles." Because I love you in that really really stupid way. He's pretty smart, though, isn't he? For the son of a stupid mother. Three? Eight? Six?

PETER Don't do this.

AMY What's she like?

PETER There is no—

[*To* JOSH.]

Go to your room.

JOSH Mom?

AMY Stay.

JOSH 'Kay.

PETER God.

[*Silence. He doesn't have an ally in the room.*]

PETER It's not—

AMY It's not what I think it is?

PETER No. It's not.

AMY You have no idea what I think.

PETER [*Holding out his cell phone.*] Here. I'll stand right here while you—

AMY Don't embarrass yourself.

PETER Go ahead. Call.

AMY Don't insult me.

[*Beat.*]

JOSH I'm gonna do it, dad. Unless you say it.

[JOSH *finally turns to face* PETER, *dead on. He waits. Nothing.*]

JOSH What is it about "now" that you don't understand?

PETER [*Snapping.*] Don't throw *my* words back in *my* face! Don't think you're so smart! Don't think for a minute—

[*He realizes he's facing his own firing squad.*]

PETER Don't.

JOSH Say "when" mom.

PETER Not now. Not in front of him. Not like this.

[*No one moves.*]

JOSH Mom?

[*Beat.*]

PETER [*Barely.*] Seven.

[JOSH *turns off the computer, sits at the dinner table and eats.*]

. . .

Fit for Feet

Jordan Harrison

Jordan Harrison

The plays of Jordan Harrison, which include *Act a Lady*, *The Museum Play*, *Kid-Simple*, and *Finn in the Underworld*, have been produced and developed at Actors Theatre of Louisville, Berkeley Repertory Theatre, Perishable Theatre, the Empty Space Theater, Playwrights Horizons, Sledgehammer Theatre, the Flea Theater, and Clubbed Thumb. *Kid-Simple* premiered at the 2004 Humana Festival and was produced in Chicago at American Theater Company. Jordan is the recipient of the Heideman Award, two Jerome Fellowships from The Playwrights' Center, and a joint commission from Children's Theatre Company and the Guthrie Theater. Jordan received his MFA in Playwriting from Brown University, and is co-editor of the annual *Play: A Journal of Plays*. A member of New Dramatists, he is represented by the William Morris Agency.

characters

CLAIRE Late twenties. Nice sweater set. Pastels.

LINDA Fifties. Improbably blonde for her age.

JIMMY Late twenties. Average Joe in a baseball cap.

A PROMINENT DANCE CRITIC Female.

Note: This play is indebted to Joan Acocella's unexpurgated edition of Nijinsky's diaries.

···scene one···

[*Stage left.* LINDA *and* CLAIRE *in Adirondack chairs.* LINDA *reclines, sipping an iced tea.* CLAIRE *sits very straight, no iced tea.*]

LINDA Isn't this civilized?

CLAIRE It is the ultimate goal of civilization to sit and do nothing.

[*This silences* LINDA *for a second.*]

LINDA How are my almost-newlyweds? How are my daughter and my wonderful new son?

CLAIRE Jimmy thinks he's Nijinsky. The dancer. [*With added difficulty.*] Recently, he's started to believe he's Nijinsky.

[*Stage right.* JIMMY *is sawing the heels off a pair of dress shoes.* CLAIRE *can see him but* LINDA *cannot.*]

LINDA Does he dance?

CLAIRE Not well, so you wouldn't think—

LINDA I adore dancing.

CLAIRE That really isn't the issue.

LINDA   The ballet in particular. Old World beauty. Strong male legs. *Lifting.*

CLAIRE   Listen to me. I think he might be losing his mind. He thinks he's a dead Russian.

LINDA   Might he be right?

CLAIRE   Jimmy has never been to Russia. He sits at a desk every day. He is not a dancer.

LINDA   [*Airily.*] We should go to the ballet.

[CLAIRE *gives her a look.*]

[*Stage right.* JIMMY *is finished with his sawing. He tries the shoes on. Success: ballet slippers.*]

LINDA   You might take a look at the seating chart. For the reception.

[*Pause.* CLAIRE *has noticed* JIMMY *putting on the "slippers."*]

LINDA   Mr. Barkley is at the same table as that Arkansas woman, and you know that won't do.

[CLAIRE *gets out of her chair and crosses to* JIMMY. *He is doing pliés now, his back to her.*]

LINDA   [*Calling after her.*] You might consider!

[LINDA *takes a resigned sip of iced tea. Her light fades*].

CLAIRE   Can I ask what you're doing?

[JIMMY *stops cold, but doesn't turn around. We can see that there is music in his head.*]

JIMMY My head's full of strange names. Diaghilev, Stravinsky, Ballet Russes. Romola, Kyra, Kostrovsky. But above all, Diaghilev. How I hate that diseased dog, and love him. As I love all God's creations.

[He begins a different exercise].

CLAIRE Did anything happen recently, anything out of the ordinary?

[He turns to her.]

JIMMY What is ordinary?

CLAIRE Did you get hit on the head, did you cross a black cat, did you limbo a ladder?

JIMMY There was the thing with the lightning.

CLAIRE What with what?

JIMMY I was walking along, minding my business—

CLAIRE *[gravely.]* That's how these things happen.

JIMMY When out of the sky—

CLAIRE Of course.

JIMMY Would you mind not—

CLAIRE Sorry.

JIMMY Last Thursday. There hadn't been rain in the forecast, but I'm coming back from work—wouldn't you know, the sky is practically black. Jet black clouds, ions crashing in the air.

CLAIRE Were you wearing your wedding shoes?

JIMMY I figure I'll make it home in time if I take the shortcut through the field.

[CLAIRE's head in her hands.]

On my way I see a cat up a tree, calico a few branches up. I start to climb, here kitty kitty, the storm all around me now. Then the Kaboom.

CLAIRE You didn't tell me this last Thursday.

JIMMY [*A sudden, regal change, evidenced in his posture.*]

Thursday, Friday. All is the same in the great wheel of life.

CLAIRE Why Nijinsky? That's what I don't get. Why not Nureyev, Baryshnikov, one of the other Kovs?

JIMMY [*Speaking of himself in the third person.*] Nijinsky is the best.

CLAIRE You're not the best.

JIMMY Wait and see.

[*Stage left. Lights rise on* LINDA.]

LINDA You're hard on him, maybe that's it.

CLAIRE I don't want there to be any illusions…

[CLAIRE *returns to her chair.*]

LINDA Wait till you're married a year. Then you can turn shrew.

CLAIRE …Any secrets. It's destructive.

LINDA Letting that lady minister do your vows—*that's* destructive.

CLAIRE We can still call the whole thing off.

[LINDA *removes a flask from her purse and pours something in her iced tea. She drinks deeply.*]

LINDA You left the iron on this morning.

CLAIRE Oopsie.

LINDA While you were dashing out.

CLAIRE Good thing you saw it then.

[*Stage right.* JIMMY *is drawing in a notebook with a crayon. Very heavily—the crayon is soon down to a stub.*]

LINDA Exactly, good thing. Or what would have happened, Claire. You might take a moment to consider.

[CLAIRE *doesn't take a moment.*]

CLAIRE The house would burn, the firemen would come, we arrive home to a charred black mess. You meet a kind fireman: big hands, a good cook. I hear those men are always good cooks. And I won't have to look after you ever again. Jimmy and I go live in some foreign, sun-dappled place. Help me find some oily rags, some lighter fluid. We'll do it right now.

LINDA You haven't considered at all.

CLAIRE I'm kind of preoccupied.

LINDA Consider. Think of Muffin, for starters.

[*Sound of a yippy dog yipping. They look off stage and back, quickly.*]

CLAIRE We would grieve.

LINDA The photographs. Everything your memory has come to rely on, melted down to a bubbling chemical ooze-thing.

CLAIRE A person can't live in the past.

LINDA The CLOTHES, Claire. You have beautiful clothes.

CLAIRE Insurance, Mother—

LINDA —Can't replace the chenille scarf.

CLAIRE Milan.

LINDA That poncho doohickey.

CLAIRE It's a *caftan*. Johannesburg.

LINDA Earrings.

CLAIRE Antique Market, Copenhagen. [*With special pride.*] I haggled.

LINDA Gorgeous.

CLAIRE I thought so.

[JIMMY *holds up his drawing, proudly, for the audience: many pairs of menacing eyes, peering out of darkness.*]

LINDA Have you considered? The absolute destruction of all you've collected, all we've amassed that makes us us. All it takes is one everyday carelessness and POOF—what do you have, who ARE you now?

[CLAIRE *sees* JIMMY'*s drawing.*]

CLAIRE I guess I hadn't considered.

[*Blackout.*]

· · · mini-Interlude · · ·

[JIMMY *performs a demented little solo here between the two scenes. He begins very awkwardly, but grows in confidence, until there is a vigorous assurance to his movements. (But he never ceases to be an average guy dancing ballet.* **Not** *Nijinsky.)*]

··· scene two ···

[CLAIRE *and* LINDA *in the Adirondack chairs, as before. They are examining* JIMMY's *drawing.*]

LINDA   Are those eyes?

CLAIRE   It's supposed to be soldiers, he told me.

LINDA   How creative.

CLAIRE   He's worse, I think. The other day I was all, "Darling, would you take a look at these china patterns?"

[JIMMY *enters. He flings off his baseball cap, a romantic gesture—his hair smoothed off his forehead. Dapper. He acts out* CLAIRE's *narrative.*]

CLAIRE   He walked up to me, looking me in the eye the whole time, grabbed my wrist, said:

JIMMY   I am noise. I am youth. I am a great hammer.

CLAIRE   Normally if a guy said that to me, *especially* my husband, I'd be: "Yeah sure, you're a hammer. Now about these patterns." But he looks at me that new way and says:

JIMMY   I am a rebel angel, Romola. You are a lusterless moon. You are fit for my feet.

CLAIRE   And he holds me and calls me by that strange name and I am *happy* to be fit for his feet.

LINDA   Susan Faludi wouldn't approve, Claire.

CLAIRE   [*In his grip.*] There's more. We're still in this violent, like, erotic, like, *clench* and he says:

JIMMY   I am God in my prick. God is in me and I am in God.

CLAIRE [*Catching her breath.*] Say that again?

JIMMY I am in God.

CLAIRE No, the other.

JIMMY I am God in my prick.

CLAIRE [*Pouncing on him.*] That's the one.

LINDA You must be delighted.

CLAIRE Delighted?

[JIMMY *crawls out from under* CLAIRE *and exits. She watches him leave.*]

It's true, I can't help but find him somewhat more...magnetic these days. This new confidence. Practicing jetés instead of scratching his pits.

LINDA I'm not sure what you're complaining about.

CLAIRE I don't *recognize* him. We're about to tell each other for better or for worse and I don't know who he is.

LINDA Can we ever *know* a person, really? Why not be married to someone who wakes up different every morning? Every day a surprise.

CLAIRE I chose *Jimmy*. That's what I want to wake up to. And maybe, every now and then, the virile and commanding Russian can come to visit.

LINDA You were always the idealist, Claire.

CLAIRE [*To herself.*] Maybe if I knew more about him.

LINDA You've dated for it's been years.

CLAIRE Nijinsky, I mean. If I did some research. Maybe this would make sense, if only we knew more.

[*A PROMINENT DANCE CRITIC enters. Haughty and urbane, she wears a dramatic, asymmetrical tunic. She reaches into the air and pulls down a white screen, center stage, without missing a beat. A slide of Nijinsky, in his famous* Afternoon of a Faun *garb, appears.*]

CRITIC Tragically, we lack a celluloid record of Nijinsky in performance.

But we know from first-hand accounts—among them, that of his great countryman Vladimir Nabokov—that when he leapt in the air, he seemed to hover for a moment, as if suspended by a gold thread leading out of his brow and through the roof.

Then, most remarkably, he lofted another inch before returning to Earth.

Every evening, audiences at the Ballets Russes witnessed an assault on the principles of gravity the like of which we haven't seen—unassisted by coarse machinery—since the Newtonian apple grounded mankind's Icarian fancies.

CLAIRE What can she mean?

LINDA Guy jumped high in the sky.

CRITIC Next slide, please.

[*The slide changes to Nijinsky, looking quite mad now, in Stravinsky's* Petrushka.]

CRITIC But if Nijinsky's leap embodied that part of us that wants to leave this world behind, it was his mind that finally carried out the dare.

CLAIRE Pardon?

CRITIC   He went positively bonkers. Abandoned by the ballet, the great
man withdrew into the pages of his diary.

Written on three notebooks in 1919, the diary evidences a mind
in which sex and war, heaven and hell simmer in the same
debauched stew. A rondo of rigmarole, penned in an uneasy
blend of his native Russian, courtly French, childlike scribblings,
and a sort of malignantly repetitive baby-talk.

Gobbledy-gook driven by a cunningly transgressive illogic.
Mother Goose gone prick-mad. Muttering, proselytizing, scato-
logically obsessed, biting the heads off crayons, Nijinsky had
become as much an animal as a God.

Is this the cost of genius? we ask the spheres.
We are still deciphering the music of their answer.

[*The* CRITIC *curtsies deeply. Her light is extinguished. The screen flies away.*]

LINDA   My head hurts.

CLAIRE   It will soon hurt more. Last night, he climbed out of bed,
sleepwalking, he does that.

[JIMMY *crosses, his arms stretched out, somnambulist-style.*]

But never like this, all the way downstairs and out the front door.
I put on a raincoat and followed him.

LINDA   A raincoat? With all your beautiful things…

CLAIRE   The most worrisome thing was he didn't trip once. Used to be
he couldn't walk for his own shoelaces. Here he was, a bounce in
his step—sidestepping cracks, sashaying past puddles, softly snor-
ing all the time. Soon we're in a part of town I've never been to.
Cobblestones, steaming potholes. Can those be gaslights?

I can't even catch sight of a Starbucks.

He seems to be practicing steps: his arms striking the air, his legs like scissors.

As I watch him, I can almost hear the music he's dancing to, and it's like he's lighter on his feet with every step.

People notice. All the motleys out at 3 a.m.:
Insomniacs with dark rings, child molesters, women with frosted hair.

[LINDA *gasps.*]

They all come out of the shadows and follow him,
They don't know why. How can they not?
Soon it's a little parade of freaks, with Jimmy at the head like a drum major.

And then he takes off.

[*Stage right.* JIMMY *leaps into the air, hovers there, and lofts another inch before landing.* CLAIRE'*s hand at her mouth.*]

I'm peeking from behind a dumpster in my old raincoat,
My hair flat around my shoulders like a wet rat.
And I don't have anything to do with that brilliant thing
in the air. And he has even less to do with Jimmy.
Enough. I break the spell, I shake him awake.
He feels small in my arms, all the people watching us.
Then his eyes open on me, ash-black, and he says "You try to keep me down..."

JIMMY [*Overlapping.*] You try to keep me down with the scalyskins and the black-eyed beasts but you are death. I am life and you are death.

LINDA One should never wake people in the middle of dreams.

CLAIRE Tomorrow we walk down the aisle and I'm *death?*

[*Stage left.* LINDA *touches* CLAIRE *on the knee.*]

LINDA I'll have a talk with him, lamb.

[*Stage right.* JIMMY *sits at a vanity, applying thick white pancake makeup. He is not effeminate about it. Rather it is a solemn ritual—putting on warpaint. Linda crosses to him.*]

LINDA Can you believe, the big day? Wait 'till you see Claire, like some kind of delicious multi-leveled parfait. All that organza—

[JIMMY *turns to her, face shocking-white.*]

LINDA Oh. [*Pause.*] Tell me my daughter's being a nervous bride. Tell me there's nothing the matter with our fine young management consultant.

JIMMY Je ne parle pas Anglais.

[*Stage left.* CLAIRE *putting on her wedding dress. Nervous.*]

LINDA You just have to parle enough to say "I do."

JIMMY Je ne parle pas Anglais.

LINDA We don't have a lot of time. Where's your tux?

JIMMY Je ne parle de plus Anglais.

LINDA [*Trying another tack.*] Je m'appelle Linda. That's all I remember from high school, can you believe?

JIMMY [*Rising.*] Je suis boeff mes pas biffstek.

LINDA Ca va bien, merci. I'm afraid that's it, my whole bag of tricks.

JIMMY [*Very close to her, a forceful whisper.*]

Je ne suis pas biffstek.

Je suis stek sans boeuf en biff.

LINDA Oh my my my. Ou est la Tour Eiffel?

JIMMY [*Slapping his thighs percussively with each "si."*]

Je ne suis je un tamboure.

Je suis si si si si si si si

LINDA [*Smoldering now.*] Un pain au chocolat, s'il vous plait!

[JIMMY *is elsewhere, oblivious to the game.*]

JIMMY Tzi tzi tzi tzi tzi tzi tzi tzi

Je suis ça suis ça suis ça je ça

ça ça ça ça ça ça ça ça ça ça

LINDA I'm afraid I lost track.

JIMMY I am a lullabyer, I am a singer of all songs.

LINDA [*Mischievously.*] I thought you didn't parle Anglais, Frenchie.

[JIMMY *jumps. This time he does not come down.* LINDA *looks up at him in awe, mouth ajar. We can see that there is music in her head.*]

[CLAIRE *stomps over in full wedding dress.*]

LINDA Excellent young man!

CLAIRE Come down come DOWN.

[CLAIRE *jumps after* JIMMY, *her arms flailing for him. After some failed attempts, she starts to take running leaps. Not even close. She continues to jump, more and more wildly. Sound of the* Wedding March *beginning.*]

[*Light fades.*]

. . .

Perfect

Mary Gallagher

Mary Gallagher

The plays of Mary Gallagher, *Father Dreams, Little Bird, Chocolate Cake, Buddies, Dog Eat Dog, Love Minus, How to Say Goodbye, De Donde?* and *Windshook* have been published by Dramatists Play Service and produced all over the U.S. (Vineyard Theatre, Ensemble Studio Theatre, Women's Project, New York Shakespeare Festival, American Conservatory Theatre, Actors Theatre of Louisville, Hartford Stage Company, Alley Theatre, Cincinnati Playhouse, et al.); and in many other countries. *De Donde?* was published in *American Theatre* in 1989. Many of Gallagher's plays are anthologized. Her screenplays for Paramount, MGM, HBO, NBC, CBS, Lifetime and Showtime include *Nobody's Child*, co-written by Ara Watson (Writers Guild Award); *Bonds of Love* (Best TV Movie of the Year, Banff International Television Festival); *and The Passion of Ayn Rand*, (premiered at Sundance 1999, aired on Showtime, Emmy for Helen Mirren, Golden Globe for Peter Fonda.) Gallagher's fellowships and honors include the Guggenheim, the Rockefeller, the NYFA, two NEAs, an NEA/TCG Residency Grant, the Susan Smith Blackburn Prize, the Rosenthal New Play Prize, the Berrilla Kerr Award, a Luminas Award from Women in Film. She is a member of Actors & Writers and an alumna of New Dramatists, where she created the series, "Conversations with Playwrights." Her new full-length play is *I Know You're the One*.

characters

TINA

KITTY

DAN

All the characters are in their late 30s.

time

The present, after dinner.

place

A hallway or pantry at TINA and BINKY's place, with something to put stuff on and something to perch or lean on.

• • •

[TINA *and* BINKY *are entertaining* KITTY *and* DAN, *who have never met before.* BINKY *is not seen. Footsteps are heard, two pairs of high heels.* TINA *enters, followed by* KITTY, *both carrying dinner dishes which they plunk down as they talk.*]

TINA   So wadaya think?

KITTY   So far, he's fine—

TINA   I think he is perfect!

KITTY   He's great-looking, that's for sure—

TINA   My God, Kitty, *I'm* drooling! And *smart*, he's like Joe Genius at the law firm, Binky says—

KITTY   He seems like he's bright, he's read a book lately, at least—

TINA   He reads like a maniac. Like at the office, Binky says everybody's talking about who would want to try out for "Survivor: The

Galapagos," and Dan is like, "You know I was reading this *book* last night," and everyone goes, "Oh." But I mean, you *love* that.

KITTY But he's funny too. I mean I think he's said a lot of funny things tonight—

TINA Are you kidding? God, he is *hysterical*! He gets Binks laughing on the phone, like Binks can't stop, like with *tears* –

KITTY And he offered to help clear the table.

TINA *That*, I could not believe.

KITTY Of course, he *is* a guest—

TINA But *still*. They *won't*, you know?

KITTY It's like the last bastion, the Alamo—

TINA Or even if they did it for some brief exciting era, now it's over. You get up, you pick up a plate, and they dig in, they get this look, this *rigid* look...

KITTY Sort of daunted, but entrenched...

TINA And they start talking sports.

KITTY Or corporate talk. "To the best of my knowledge, Fred."

TINA Right! Right! That's the best thing about Binky being Binky. When people start that crap with him, it just doesn't cut it. "To the best of my knowledge, Binky..."

[*They start giggling. They lean on each other, giggling. DAN enters.*]

DAN Hey.

TINA Hey.

KITTY   Hey.

DAN   You guys are having a good time in here. Binks and I are missing it. We feel ripped off. We feel we should express that.

KITTY   And we're glad you did.

[*He keeps looking at her for a beat. There is clearly a strong mutual attraction. They are faintly smiling.* TINA *enjoys this. Then:*]

DAN   Also, Binky sent me to inquire, I quote, "What is the coffee situation?"

TINA   It's working, tell him. What's he think this is, the Dog 'n Suds?

DAN   Uh...

TINA   He's the one that bought the espresso-maker, so he's gotta learn to wait. Tell him to pretend he's in, you know, whatsit—

KITTY/DAN   Tuscany.

TINA   Tuscany.

DAN   How 'bout if I tell him it's almost ready?

KITTY   "To the best of my knowledge, Binky."

DAN   [*Grins.*] "Just an estimate, based on available data—we'll crunch more numbers, Binks."

[DAN *exits. They listen for a beat till he's gone. Then* TINA *pokes* KITTY.]

TINA   [*About the vibes.*] WOO!

KITTY   Yeah. It's great. So far.

TINA   What is this "so far"? There is no hidden horror. Trust me. I told you, I looked into him. Not only is he not attached, he has the perfect history. He was married once, so he's not afraid of com-mitment. But they were really young and it just didn't work out. But they're still friends, he even plays squash with her new hus-band, so clearly he's not bitter. *But,* they've been divorced for *years,* and he's dated a lot and lived with two other women, so he's not hung up on her. No kids, so there is no issue of "maybe his kids will hate you." But he has one nephew and two nieces and he adores them, so he's not *opposed* to kids. *Plus* he doesn't smoke, he drinks like just enough, he gets loose but not sloppy, and he'll smoke some dope if someone passes it around, but he doesn't *buy* dope and even when he smokes it, he never turns into an asshole. I mean, if you don't take him, take Binky and *I'll* take him!

KITTY   I really am attracted to him—

TINA   Tell me about it! It's like…a force!

KITTY   Yeah?

TINA   Yeah! Also you keep grinning.

KITTY   I do? Oh God—

TINA   You both do. Me and Binky feel left out.

KITTY   God, how embarrassing—

TINA   So what's the hold-up?

KITTY   [*Beat, then.*] You're gonna get pissed off.

TINA   I might, I'll tell ya. I oughta get annointed Queen for coming up with him. Or Pope. 'Cause do you know what's *out there?*

KITTY   I know, I know, believe me…Okay. Look at the evidence. He's a corporate lawyer. He makes a lot of money.

TINA   It's not that great, he makes like what Binky makes—

KITTY   Compared to say the average income of the average working—

TINA   Okay, okay, right—

KITTY   He drives a BMW. He went to Fiji on vacation. He makes jokes about his investment portfolio, but he *has* a portfolio and he's only, what? Thirty-six?

TINA   Thirty-eight. That's better, men are assholes till they're thirty-eight. See, he's even thirty-eight! *What are you afraid of?*

KITTY   Who do you think he voted for?

TINA   [*Stopped; then stalls for time.*] Huh?

KITTY   I knew it!

TINA   No no, wait, hold on—

KITTY   God, it's all so *depressing*—

TINA   No, wait a minute, we don't know—

KITTY   You know, you know in your heart—

TINA   I don't! You *never* know. Binky's just the same as Dan, he's practically a clone of Dan, and Binky didn't vote for him—

KITTY   That's because you told him if he voted for him, he would not get laid for four more years.

TINA   But he wouldn't've done it anyway, Binky never *really* votes for them. Sometimes, yeah, he talks the talk, just to get me all wound up, but "once inside the booth," you know—

KITTY   This is denial, Tina.

TINA No! Even when Reagan died, the Great Communicator and the state funeral and all, and everyone kept saying, "Ronald Reagan made us feel good about ourselves again," and then they'd play these soundbites from his speeches? And Binky said, "Tina, listen to his voice, he sounds like a child molester."

[*Doing creepy Reagan.*]

"Come with me, little girl, it's morning in America…"

KITTY Yeah, yeah…we can all sneer and laugh at them, but do you think they care? They sell yo-yos in the gift shop of the Ronald Reagan Presidential Library, *yo-yos* with Ronald Reagan's name on them, that's how much they care.

TINA All I'm saying is, Binky doesn't vote for them—

KITTY It's how Dan votes that worries me!

TINA Well, I don't think it's fair. For you to just…assume…

KITTY I bet Binky knows.

TINA [*Lying.*] …I don't think they talk politics.

KITTY Get Binky and I'll ask him.

TINA Oh, great, that's great! Why don't you just ask Dan? Go ahead, just…

[*Throws up hands.*]

KITTY [*Bleakly.*] Because if he votes for them, I'll cry, or puke, or something…

TINA [*Beat; then, gently.*] Look. Why don't you wait. You know? Enjoy it for a while. You guys could have so much fun. And he could be the greatest lover in America. Don't ruin it before you even—

KITTY No, I can't face falling for him, getting suckered in, but all the time suspecting, probing, and then finding out! No. I'd rather end it now. One clean…

[*Chopping motion.*]

I'll go back in, I'll ask him.

[KITTY *turns to exit.* TINA *grabs her.*]

TINA Now, dammit, Kitty! This is really self-destructive. I don't think you *want* to have a good relationship. Or even a good time! I think…I think, and I am serious, you are *avoiding* real live men—

KITTY No! There are certain things—principles, gut instincts, call them what you will—that every person has to cling to. That's what makes us who we are. I would not ask *you* to give up the deepest convictions that you have—

TINA [*Annoyed.*] Name one!

KITTY —and you would not want <u>me</u> to throw away my most dearly-held beliefs—

TINA I want you to have a nice man in your life! I want you to be happy!

KITTY …Yeah, I know. And I want that too, I do! But I can't stand the way this country's going. And if I can't stop it, at least I won't participate. I won't have sex with anyone who votes for them.

TINA [*Beat, then, flatly.*] You're talking about every man who makes a decent living—

KITTY No!

TINA Well, the vast majority—

KITTY No! No! In 2000, Bush didn't even win! He sneaked in the back door because his brother's flunkies blinded senior citizens and wouldn't let black people vote!

TINA Oh God, here we go...

KITTY And how about all those people who stopped voting *years* ago, because they were too weak and wasted, *drained*, from all those years of *rage* to drag their bodies to the polls! Worn out by years of Reagan and Old Bad Bush and Ollie North and Newt Gingrich and Trent Lott and *Antonin Scalia, God!* And it just gets more horrendous, now it's George the Worst! And Cheney, Rumsfeld, Rove, Rice—

TINA Whoa, whoa, didn't you just skip eight years? Clinton was one of ours. And the guy would screw a canteloupe.

KITTY Clinton broke our hearts, but getting blowjobs at the office is not the same as throwing out social security so that we can spend our golden years living in cardboard cartons!

TINA Don't ask Dan tonight, okay, I don't need a bloodbath here—

KITTY Clinton didn't try to give away the arctic wilderness! He didn't call an education bill "No Child Left Behind" and then leave behind the funding! He didn't bring back Star Wars and gag orders for birth control and trillion dollar deficits! He didn't lock up immigrants for years just "on suspicion," without lawyers or human rights! He didn't attack a *country* just so he could carve it up and hand the pieces to his friends and act like no one's dying! And Clinton could speak in *sentences*, with *clauses*. He could sustain a complex thought! Bush is a vacuum, a black hole, I'm surprised the Lincoln bed doesn't get sucked into him—

[DAN *enters.* KITTY *shuts up. They look at each other, slowly start smiling.* TINA *grins.*]

TINA   I think the coffee's ready.

[TINA *exits.*]

DAN   Want to have dinner tomorrow night?

KITTY   [*beat, then blurts*] Did you vote for Bush?

DAN   [*surprised*] Actually, I didn't vote. Terrible, I know. But the firm packed me off to Kuwait with one day's notice, so I didn't have time to do the absentee ballot thing.

KITTY   Oh...huh...

[*She's more torn: can she let it go at this? She and DAN slowly move toward each other as:*]

I would like to have dinner with you.

DAN   Great.

KITTY   I really want to have sex with you.

DAN   Fantastic.

[*They move into their first kiss. But* KITTY *breaks it, she can't help herself.*]

KITTY   But if you *had* voted, who would you have voted for?

[*Blackout.*]

• • •

The Wounded Do Not Cry

**A play inspired
by the life of
Frances Slanger,
forgotten heroine
of Normandy.**

Lavonne Mueller

Lavonne Mueller

As a Woodrow Wilson Visiting Scholar, Lavonne Mueller has helped colleges around the United States set up writing programs. She has been an Arts America speaker for the USIS (United States Information Services) in India, Finland, Romania, Japan, the former Yugoslavia, and Norway. She was recently a Fulbright Fellow to Jordan and also received a National Endowment for the Humanities Grant to do research in Paris during the summer of 1995. She has been a writing fellow at the Edward Albee Foundation, the Djerassi Foundation, Hawthorden Castle, and Funduncio Valperasio in Spain. She has edited three books of monologues for Heinemann: *Baseball Monologues*, *Elvis Monologues*, and *Monologues from the Road*. Her play *American Dreamers* was selected for the book *Best American Short Plays: 1995–1996*, Applause Books. Her play, *The Confession of Many Strangers*, was produced at the White Barn Theatre and has been published in *Best American Short Plays: 1998* (Applause Books) as well as Oxford Press. Her play *Carrying the Light*, opened in Tokyo on November 15, 2000. Her textbook on creative writing is published by Doubleday/National Textbook Company. Her play *Hotel Splendid*, was presented in New York City in 2003 by Multistages at the Dramatist Guild. *Hotel Splendid* was published in English and Korean and the book received the 2003 Award for outstanding drama opposing war and injustice, given by Peacewriting and sponsored by the Consortium of Peace, Research and Development (COPRED).

characters

FRANCES   age 31

IRENE   age 26

One male actor plays the parts of:

OFFICER, DOCTOR, LT. STEIN.

time

June 10, 1944. 2 pm

place

The Normandy Invasion

. . .

[*We hear artillery shells.*]

VOICE OVER: Now hear this! Now hear this! The William N. Pendleton U.S. Merchant Marine Ship: All troops to your debarkation areas! All troops to your debarkation areas!

[*As lights go up, we see projected on a wall of paper the famous picture of MacArthur wading through water as he returns to the Philippines.*
We hear louder shelling.
Frances suddenly breaks through the wall of paper with the picture of MacArthur and comes center stage in a field jacket, canvas life belt, and oversized helmet, all distressed by the water and debris off Normandy. She struggles in the water, bobbing up and down.
Lights up immediately on a U.S. Army OFFICER on a higher level of the stage. He's standing against a battleship railing.]

OFFICER   She's no MacArthur. Anyway, the General lands months later on the Philippines…taking 30 or 40 long strides in water up to his knees.

FRANCES [*Ignoring officer's comment as she holds out her dog tag to display.*]

I'm Lt. Frances Y. Slanger, U.S. Army Nurse Corps. Landing on Normandy. With water over my head.

OFFICER What I want to know is…what's the Kike doing here?

[FRANCES *pauses, hears this but doesn't look at the officer. Lights out on the officer.*]

[IRENE, *another nurse, now comes through the hole in the paper-wall to join Frances. Irene wades in water as if in slow motion.*]

IRENE Frances…Frances…this way. The Forty-Fifth they said is this way.

FRANCES My legs are itchy from the salt water.

IRENE Thank heavens my lipstick is wrapped in plastic.

FRANCES [*Pause. Looks back.*] Where is everybody?

IRENE Keep paddling!

FRANCES Eisenhower said we're embarking on the Great Crusade, Irene.

IRENE Did he mention that sea water's bad for the hair?

FRANCES He just said: Send the nurses to Normandy.

IRENE Be careful…the Germans sometimes bulldoze furrows in the water. The depth can drop from chest-high to ten feet.

FRANCES Ok…Ok.

IRENE Don't touch that thing! It's a mine lashed to the top of a pole. My boyfriend told me about these.

FRANCES Which boyfriend?

IRENE Sailor Bob.

[*They struggle in the water.*]

FRANCES Why didn't we learn to dog paddle at Fort Devins?

IRENE We were too busy learning how to dodge bullets.

FRANCES I've got Keats under my helmet.

IRENE It'll take more than any Keats to stop bullets.

[*They struggle in the water.*]

FRANCES There's…dead bodies floating by me.

IRENE Frances, there will be hundreds more to come.

FRANCES I'm going to help them.

IRENE Don't touch that boot! Let it go by.

FRANCES But Irene…there's part of a leg still in it.

IRENE We're only a few yards from the beach. Frances…Frances…

[IRENE *grabs* FRANCES *and* FRANCES' *head comes up out of the water as* FRANCES *spits out water.*]

FRANCES I'm ok. Just gulped a little water.

IRENE When we hit the beach, we hook up with the men.

FRANCES Where are the rest of us nurses?

IRENE Waiting for two slowpokes.

FRANCES I can't see the beach.

IRENE It's there. Murky looking from the heat. Now let's go. Double time!

[*They struggle in the water and then finally fall flat on the beach gasping.*]

IRENE And I dreamed of wearing one of those cute starched white nurse's hats.

FRANCES My hair's too frizzy to wear under any starched hat.

IRENE Mine isn't. [*Pause.*] See anybody?

FRANCES Not yet. [*Pause.*] I look good in a helmet. Makes my eyes bigger.

> [IRENE *takes off her helmet and we see her hair is in large metal rollers.*]

FRANCES You…look like…a Picasso.

IRENE Is that a good thing?

FRANCES "Nothing's good or bad but thinking makes it so."

IRENE Do you have to sound like a poet during this invasion?

[FRANCES *screams.*]

IRENE What's wrong?

FRANCES [*Happily.*] You called me a poet.

IRENE It's enough to be a nurse.

[*We hear artillery shells.*]

IRENE

> [*Puts her helmet on as they both duck down.*]

Now that's something to scream about.

IRENE Why did I think this job would be glamorous?

FRANCES Irene, whoever said war was glamorous?

IRENE For one, it's that war poet you're always reading. What's his name....Owen?

FRANCES I'm not doing this because of him. I'm here to stop the Nazis.

IRENE Before we do that, I'd like to take down my curlers.

[*They cautiously look up.*]

FRANCES Where is everybody?

IRENE Guess we drifted off to the north.

FRANCES Way down there...see all that...driftwood?

IRENE Don't look, Frances.

FRANCES Are those...?

IRENE We've got to find the hospital.

FRANCES Oh, god, what's happening here?

IRENE We're at the front, Frances.

FRANCES Are the other nurses dead, too?

IRENE They're probably hooked up with the men.

[*Light up on a doctor who is a captain.*]

DOCTOR Girls. Over here!

[*They walk to the hospital area.*]

FRANCES Where are the other nurses?

DOCTOR Helping bring in the wounded.

IRENE [*Taking down her curlers.*] Any clean uniforms?

DOCTOR   Push those two footlockers together.

[IRENE *and* FRANCES *push the two footlockers together.*]

FRANCES   [*To* DOCTOR:] For your instruments?

DOCTOR   For my patients. I'll soon be up to my neck in surgery.

FRANCES   This is an operating table?

DOCTOR   Where the hell are you from, little girl?

FRANCES   Boston.

DOCTOR   You want Boston General hospital here?

IRENE   [*weakly*] I'm from...Illinois.

DOCTOR   Illinois, now. Expect Michael Reese Hospital?

IRENE   Paw Paw, Illinois.

DOCTOR   Greenhorns. Why me!

FRANCES   We're both fully qualified graduates of...

DOCTOR   Yah...yah. Look for flashlights. Supply dumped them somewhere around here.

FRANCES   Flashlights?

DOCTOR   Need light to operate. Even in Boston, they got to have light.

IRENE   This is the...Forty-Fifth Field Hospital?

DOCTOR   You're looking at him.

FRANCES   They said there'd be generators.

DOCTOR   Who said that? The recruiting officer? [*He laughs.*]

Flashlight, girls.

[IRENE *and* FRANCES *look around the area.*]

DOCTOR We're expecting 10,000 dead. The dead we don't worry about. Now the hundreds of wounded...

FRANCES Hundreds?

DOCTOR Mangled hundreds.

IRENE Any other doctors?

DOCTOR Suppose to be some on the way. Who knows when.

DOCTOR [*He takes a flashlight out of the box, tries to turn it on as it lays limp and unlighted in his hand.*]

I believe I said...we don't bother with the dead.

[FRANCES *stares at him.*]

DOCTOR They have batteries in Boston? In Pow Wow, Illinois?

IRENE Paw Paw.

DOCTOR Batteries! Little girls, if there are flashlights, can batteries be far behind?

[IRENE *and* FRANCES *look around for the box of batteries.*]

DOCTOR When you get time, hang some lanterns, too. And put up the mosquito netting. I want all the glass syringes boiled. And ladies...if you need the latrine, there's a slit-trench on the left side of our tent. A private will be stationed out there to issue you three squares of toilet paper per visit.

[IRENE *and* FRANCES *stare at each other.*]

[*Sound of trucks is heard.*]

DOCTOR Here they come!

[*Light out on the doctor as he exits.* IRENE *and* FRANCES *come forward and sit on the floor together.*]

IRENE [*Fanning herself with a large bandage.*] The air's stifling in this tent.

    [*Pause.*]

    Getting any sleep?

FRANCES I was in surgery all night.

[*Sound of distant artillery.*]

IRENE [*About artillery:*] That bother you?

FRANCES I pretend it's the elevated trains from South Port Station near my house in Boston.

IRENE The one thing that really gets to me…

FRANCES …when the German planes fly over?

IRENE Trying to take a bath in a helmet full of rainwater, twigs and worms.

FRANCES I dream about soap.

IRENE Oh, I finally got some.

FRANCES Where?

IRENE From one of the medics who got a package from home. He wanted two bucks for it, but I'm so broke, I jewed him down to one.

    [*A strained beat as* IRENE *realizes what she said. She stares at*

FRANCES, *her lips trying to form an apology, but nothing comes out. Finally:*]

FRANCES I'm tight as a Scotchman, myself.

[*They both laugh.*]

IRENE Frances, did you always want to be a nurse?

FRANCES Sure. You?

IRENE In third grade a little boy smashed his finger on the jungle bars. I wrapped my hankie around his pinkie. He looked at me with adoring eyes. I figured…good way to get a guy's attention. And here I am. What got you going?

FRANCES A pear.

IRENE A pair of good biceps, huh?

FRANCES My dad's a fruit peddler in South Boston.

IRENE No kidding.

FRANCES I helped him since I was seven. [*Pause.*] We always took such pride stacking the fruit…polishing apples to put their cheeks next to steps of golden oranges…weaving lace of purple and green grapes along the side. Then…a big juicy pear on top. But there were kids who didn't like us, and they'd knock over our cart. Once…the pear rolled away…it's flesh all torn.

[*She reaches for a stone on the beach as if it were the pear.*]

I tried pushing all the pulp back together.

[*She squeezes the stone.*]

I wanted to make it better…make it whole again.

[*She squeezes the stone harder.*]

I wanted it...perfect...like it was.

IRENE [*Tries to get* FRANCES *to release her hold on the stone.*]

Good lord, Frances, that's a sharp stone. Come on, let go.

FRANCES Fruit has such a short life....and crooks had to smash it....bigots had to kill it.

IRENE Drop it...Frances, it's like a knife...your hand's starting to bleed.

SHOUTS OF: Nurse! Nurse! Nurse!

[IRENE *exits. A pause as* FRANCES *drops the stone on the ground and wipes her blood stained hands on the side of her uniform and then goes to the ward of the wounded. She stands in the middle of the stage surrounded by agonizing shouts of: Nurse! Nurse!*]

[FRANCES *goes to the cot of one wounded soldier.*]

FRANCES [*She takes his temperature.*]

Good. You're down to 101 today.

[*She goes to another cot carrying a towel over her arm.*]

FRANCES I'm going to give you a new wonder drug—Pencillin. You'll be up and around in no time. What? Yes. Yes. I've taken care of your friends...they're fine. No, I didn't let them see the medicine I'm giving you. That's right, we don't want to alarm them. See, I've hidden the syringe under my towel.

[*She now gives him a shot.*]

[*She goes to another cot with a soldier with a head bandage.*]

Your bandage needs tightening. Here, I'll just pull this closer. Tonight, I'll come back and read your wife's letter to you.

[*She goes to another cot.*]

You must eat. I know C-rations aren't too delicious. But you must eat. Let me put some mash potatoes on your tongue. Take a little...please...just a little. Good...good. That's it. If you taste something sweet you're probably biting into a worm. Not to worry. The worm's cooked long enough to be sterilized. [*Chuckles.*]

[*She looks out over all the cots.*]

I know...I know...all of you want banana cream pie. Well I'd give anything to see a fat chicken on a platter for Shabbat dinner, myself.

[*She turns to the next patient in the next cot as light goes up on* IRENE.]

IRENE Frances...that's a German soldier. They found him on the beach.

FRANCES Irene, we need more cotton.

IRENE Frances, I can take care of him for you.

FRANCES We're winning the war. I can afford a dose of compassion.

[*To the German soldier:*]

I'm just pouring sulfanilamide powder on your wounds. It will help fight the infection. [*Pause.*] What?

[*She puts her ear down next to his lips.*]

Yes. Juden. I'm 2nd Lt. Freidel Yachet Schlanger, United States Army Nurse Corps.

[*She powders his wounds.* FRANCES *then turns to another soldier as* IRENE *calls to her:*]

IRENE Frances, where did you get that box of surgical gloves and extra bed pans?

FRANCES [*As she is bandaging a patient:*]
Doc sent me up the road to the Supply Hut.

IRENE That's dangerous. The road's plastered with mines.

FRANCES Doc just said: Look for chickens. If they're clucking and alive, the area is probably safe from mines.

[*Light out on* IRENE.]

[*Light up on the doctor.*]

DOCTOR Treat all casualties quickly and silently. There's no time to waste. Take no histories. Act like a veterinarian.

FRANCES I have a dog back home, Doctor. When he's sick, I treat him like any other patient.

DOCTOR There will be plenty of time for all that after the war.

FRANCES I'll make plenty of time for it now.

DOCTOR Just see that you keep up. And Frances, wait until the scalpel hits the flesh before you give ether. We can't afford to waste any.

[*Lights out on* DOCTOR. *Light remains on* FRANCES *as she takes paper and pencil out of her pocket to write a letter.*]

FRANCES Dear Mama and Papa, I know you are unhappy about me being so far away. But didn't you both leave Poland and travel to America?

[*Pause.*]

So you've heard about the Invasion. And they rang the church bells at 3 a.m. in Boston. I'm happy to know my Mama and Papa knelt on our front porch at 3 a.m. in their nightclothes and prayed for us here.

[*Pause.*]

I wash soldiers. Give morphine shots. Bandage wounds. Put kidney basins under bleeding chins.

[*Pause.*]

They brought in a 20-year-old boy, a bullet in both arms. He wanted me to patch him up in a hurry so he could grab his gun and go back into battle. I tried to calm him...put cold cloths on his forehead...rubbed his back...even as the doctor stood behind him ready to amputate both his arms.

[FRANCES *takes a sock out of her pocket. Light up on* IRENE *who is holding two towels.*]

IRENE   Frances, what are you doing?

FRANCES   I'm hungry.

IRENE   I guess a sock can be filling.

FRANCES   I put a can of C-rations in the sock. Lower it into a tin of hot water. These beach twigs all around here make a nice fire.

IRENE   We're suppose to be swimming...resting...cooking ain't resting. Eat a pack of C-crackers.

[*She throws* FRANCES *a towel.*]

FRANCES   I threw away all my canned peaches and pears. I've had enough of fruit. [*Pause.*] Beef stew. I eat it sticking the end of my toothbrush into the meat. I won't know how to use a fork after the war. [*Pause.*] They brought in a corporal today who was trying to stuff his intestines back into his stomach.

IRENE Let get our toes wet. It's safe in this little cove. And a 20-millimeter bullet can't go deeper than 6 feet.

FRANCES How do you know that?

IRENE My boyfriend told me.

FRANCES Not Sailor Bob, again?

IRENE Artillery Tom. Come on, we'll swim low.

FRANCES Stacks of bones. That's all they bring us, Irene. Flesh burned off by flame throwers. "What passing bells for those who die as cattle."

[FRANCES *stands.*]

I'm tired of death. Tired! What good are we doing? They just keep coming....there's no end to it. I want to go home.

[*She begins to cry.*]

IRENE [*Puts her arms around* FRANCES.]

We all want that. All of us. Soldiers. Doctors. Nurses. The poor French people driven from their homes. Roosevelt's four sons over here. [*Pause.*] That little French girl they brought in this morning? You were so good with that kid.

FRANCES Danielle.

IRENE You patched her up...taking shrapnel out of her leg so she didn't even cry.

FRANCES I gave her ether as soon as I lay her down.

IRENE See. We need you. I would have waited until...

FRANCES/IRENE TOGETHER   ...the scalpel hit the flesh.

IRENE   Somebody around here has to break the rules. Now jump in. The water will soothe you. We'll close our eyes and just float.

VOICES OF SOLDIERS   Nurse! Nurse! Nurse!

[FRANCES *and* IRENE *go to the soldiers.*]

FRANCES   [*Bending over a soldier on a cot.*]
A splintered bone has cut an artery, lieutenant.

LT. STEIN   Am I...going to live?

FRANCES   I'm pressing my finger on your artery. That stops the bleeding.

LT. STEIN   My buddies...

FRANCES   You don't want to worry them. Irene, can you put a screen around us.

IRENE   [*As she puts the screen around them and softly in an aside so the soldier can't hear:*] The severed artery is too deep.

[IRENE *exits.*]

FRANCES   So, Lt. Stein, where do you come from?

LT. STEIN   "Much have I travell'd in the realms of gold."

FRANCES   "And many goodly states and kingdoms seen."

LT. STEIN   You like Keats, too.

FRANCES   He helps me dodge bullets...so I can carry on here...even write a little poetry.

LT. STEIN   [*Pause as the lieutenant groans.*]

Nurse. I know I'm done for. How much longer do I have?

FRANCES As long as my finger's here, Lt. Stein!

LT. STEIN I know it's bad. I could feel the bullets stitching me down the back.

FRANCES But you can still speak poetry.

LT. STEIN "Having seen all things red/Their eyes are rid/Of the hurt of the colour of blood forever." Wilfred Owen. [*Pause.*] Know the best way to water geraniums?

FRANCES With the garden hose?

LT. STEIN Naw. You make tea to water geraniums. My Mom taught me that…and when I was laying on the field…before they picked me up….I could see her…right in front of me with the tea kettle. [*Pause.*] Have you seen my buddy? Wade Dutter? We're from the same town. Whitefish, Montana. He was right next to me when…

FRANCES I'll look for him.

LT. STEIN He picked up a lot of bullets in his gear. So maybe he's ok. It's probably good that you haven't seen him. He's younger than me. Maybe 20. Oh, God. "What passing bells for those who die as cattle."

FRANCES "The shrill, demented choirs of wailing shells." *Anthem For Doomed Youth.*

LT. STEIN You sure know your Wilfred Owen.

FRANCES He lets me see the war the way you do.

LT. STEIN Why are you here? Somebody like you?

FRANCES Reading too much Walt Whitman, I guess.

LT. STEIN Sure. Old Walt nursed the wounded in the Civil War. "Every hour of the light and dark is a miracle/every cubic inch of space is a miracle."

[*A pause as he stares at her.*]

LT. STEIN Do you really write poetry?

FRANCES Yes.

LT. STEIN Recite one.

FRANCES They're not good, Lt. Stein.

LT. STEIN Just one.

FRANCES I don't want to bore you.

LT. STEIN Please.

FRANCES [*Recites:*]

> If Whitman wrapped your head
> in white flags of bandages
> he'd soothe that black space
> in the corner of your soul's face
> and you could reach peace
> that Americans sings of
> each to each.

LT. STEIN [*After a pause.*] I...like that. You should send it to *Stars and Stripes* so the troops can read it.

FRANCES Not too many poetry loving GI's like us, Lt. Stein.

LT. STEIN [*Groans in pain.*] Nurse...you can be honest with me...Whitman to Whitman. I know the score.

[*Lights up on* IRENE.]

IRENE   Frances, we got orders to move out. All the patients are loaded up.

LT. STEIN   We're the last ones, Nurse. My buddies won't see me die.

FRANCES   And I won't either.

IRENE   The trucks are waiting.

FRANCES   Lieutenant, just what kind of tea for those flowers?

LT. STEIN   A gentle kind.

FRANCES   I would think....Camomile.

LT. STEIN   You.... must save...yourself.

IRENE   We got to leave, now!

FRANCES   "Nothing is good or bad but thinking makes it so." Now we're with Shakespeare, Lieutenant Stein.

[*Light out on* IRENE.]

[LT. STEIN *groans in pain and lapses into unconsciousness.*]

[*The sound of trucks leaving. we see fatigued* FRANCES *holding on, her finger pressed stubbornly on the artery. Then we hear heavy artillery fire. Then louder artillery fire.* FRANCES *slumps over the soldier, her finger finally letting go as her body goes limp.*]

[*Lights up on* IRENE.]

IRENE   [*She is holding* FRANCES' *helmet.*]

After our patients were safely in a new area, we came back for Frances...and did everything we could for her. But she was hemorrhaging. The doctor and I were unable to stop the bleeding in her stomach. [*Pause.*] She died at age 31 on October 21, 1944. From enemy fire.

[IRENE *sets* FRANCES' *helmet on an IV pole center stage.*]

IRENE   A black soldier played taps. And I sent off one of her poems. *Stars and Stripes* published it.

[*Voice of* FRANCES *as the lights slowly go down on* FRANCES' *helmet on the I.V. pole.*]

FRANCES' VOICE

A nurse
sees wooden bullets
that splinter
as they shoot into the skin,
waterproof bullets
where the powder's sealed
so even the moisture of blood can't get in.

In the shock ward
she sees it all
soldiers writhing in pain and thirst.
But the wounded never cry
their buddies come first.

• • •

Water Music

A short play

Tina Howe

Tina Howe

Tina Howe is the author of *The Nest, Birth and After Birth, Museum, The Art of Dining, Painting Churches, Coastal Disturbances, Approaching Zanzibar, One Shoe Off, Pride's Crossing, Such Small Hands, Rembrandt's Gift*, new translations of Eugène Ionesco's *The Bald Soprano* and *The Lesson* as well as a host of shorter plays. These works premiered at the Los Angeles Actor's Theatre, the New York Shakespeare Festival, the Kennedy Center, The Old Globe Theater, Lincoln Center Theater, Actor's Theatre of Louisville, The Second Stage and Atlantic Theatre Company.

Among her many awards are an Obie for Distinguished Playwriting, a New York Drama Critics Circle Award for *Pride's Crossing*, an Outer Critics Circle Award, a Rockefeller Grant, two N.E.A. Fellowships, two honorary degrees, a Guggenheim Fellowship, an American Academy of Arts and Letters Award in Literature, an American Theatre Wing Award and most recently, the 24th annual William Inge Award for Distinguished Achievement in the American Theater. In 1987, she received a Tony nomination for Best Play (*Coastal Disturbances*). Miss Howe has been a Visiting Professor at Hunter College since 1990 and has taught master classes at NYU, UCLA, Columbia and Carnegie Mellon. Her works can be read in numerous anthologies as well as in *Coastal Disturbances: Four Plays by Tina Howe, Approaching Zanzibar and Other Plays* and *Pride's Crossing*, all published by Theatre Communications Group. Miss Howe is proud to have served on the council of the Dramatists Guild since 1990.

characters

ROZ   A high school English teacher, pushing 50

JESUS   The sexy Latino life guard, early 30s

OPHELIA   Polonius' mad daughter from Hamlet, 20s

setting

The whirlpool at a neighborhood health club on the Upper West Side of New York City.

time

Yesterday

• • •

[*At rise: The rousing allegro from Suite No. 1 of Handel's* Water Music *plays.* JESUS *the life guard, sits by the 20-foot off-stage lap pool trying to stay awake. Nothing happens for several moments then* ROZ *makes her way over to the whirlpool, turns on the jets and sinks in with a contented sigh.*]

ROZ   [*Removing her cap and goggles.*]
  Fifteen minutes of continuous laps...Not bad.

[*She positions herself so that that one of the jets hits her lower back. She's in heaven, but then the temperature of the water starts to drop. She moves from jet to jet, trying to get warm.*]

ROZ   What's going on with the temperature in here? One minute it's a toasty 103 degrees and the next I feel like I'm being blended into a frozen margarita! [*Struggling to get out.*] HELLLP! HELLLLLLP!

JESUS   [Waking with a start, in Spanish:]
  Who? Where? What?

ROZ *Jesus,* Jesus!

JESUS [*Rushing over to her.*] Hay-zoos, my name is Hay-zoos!

ROZ [*Flailing her arms.*]
I DON'T CARE WHAT YOUR GODDAMNED NAME IS,
I'M LOSING ALL FEELING IN MY LEGS!

JESUS [*Helping her out.*]
HAY-zoos Eduardo de Los Angeles Avila Morales!

ROZ [*Moving stiffly.*]
Meet the Abominable Snow Woman!

JESUS [*Feeling the water.*]
It's not so cold!

ROZ What do you know about cold? You're a hot blooded Latino who grew up in some steaming tropical rain forest on the outskirts of Machu Picchu!

[*A brief silence. Then* JESUS *suddenly brings the rain forest to life, imitating chattering monkeys and screeching parrots.*]

ROZ Nice…very nice! But I'd be even more impressed if you took care of things around here!

JESUS My father taught me how to converse with all of God's creatures—from the tiny glittering butterfly to the gigantic killer whale. [*More sound effects.*]

ROZ Yeah, yeah… This whirlpool is a disgrace! If it's not freezing, it's filthy! You know what I saw floating on the bottom last week? A nest of pubic hair, a half eaten strawberry and a school of albino shrimp! They were wearing mittens. That's right. Teeny tiny *red* mittens. [*Barely audible.*] With matching scarves…! Life is hard enough without being accosted by toxic refuse! You try being an English teacher in the New York public school system for 25 years! I have bone spurs in my neck, arthritis in my knees and an asthma condition that sends me to the emergency room twice a month! I come here to get a little relief! Not to be sucked into some aberrant sewer system... If you spent less time doing laps before the club opens, you'd be more aware of what's going on in this shit hole! But no, you've got to swim just four more miles. I've never seen anyone so obsessed with swimming. Pretty soon you'll be tackling the Atlantic ocean!

JESUS   Not the Atlantic ocean, the English Channel!

ROZ   The English Channel, the Atlantic Ocean, the River Styx! What difference does it make? You're so water logged you've forgotten how to maneuver on dry land.

[*There's a celestial sound. The jets shut off, the lights flicker and we hear torrents of rushing water. OPHELIA suddenly rises out of the whirlpool. She's soaking wet, dressed in a clinging Elizabethan gown, covered with vines and wild flowers.*]

JESUS   [*Falls to his knees and starts praying in Spanish, thinking she's the Virgin Mary.*]

Hail Mary, full of grace, blessed art thou among women, and blessed is the fruit of thy womb Jesus. [*etc. etc. overlapping.*]

[*ROZ stares at her, dumbfounded. OPHELIA steps out of the pool and hands her a variety of wild flowers.*]

OPHELIA   [*Speaking with an English accent.*] "There's rosemary, that's for remembrance; pray you love, remember: and there is pansies, that's for thoughts..."

ROZ   *Ophelia?*

OPHELIA "There's fennel for you, and columbines: —there's rue for you; and here's some for me: —we may call it herb-grace o' Sundays..."

JESUS [*In Spanish*.] Forgive me, Mother for I have sinned.

[*He returns to his praying, overlapping* OPHELIA.]

ROZ *Shakespeare's Ophelia in our whirlpool.*

OPHELIA [*Handing her more flowers.*]

"O, you must wear your rue with a difference. —There's a daisy: —I would give you some violets, but they withere'd all when my father died: —they say he made a good end."

[OPHELIA *wanders around the pool softly singing to herself, as* JESUS *prays with rising terror.*]

ROZ Jesus, Hay-zoos, take it easy! It's not the Virgin Mary, it's Ophelia. You know, from *Hamlet*... "To be or not to be"... The Shakespeare play! She's a vision, an apparition... Like how the Virgin Mary shows up from time to time. But she's not *actually* the Virgin Mary, but a sort of stand in, a kind of... understudy. But Ophelia showing up is *truly* miraculous because she never existed! She's just a character in a play!

[JESUS *starts beating himself with a towel.*]

ROZ You do know who Ophelia is, don't you? Hamlet's girlfriend who went mad and drowned herself after he accidentally killed her father....One minute he's swearing eternal love to her and the next he's raving like a maniac! *The poor thing never had a chance!* He used her!

[OPHELIA *finishes her song and stops dead. She gazes at them, totally disoriented.*]

ROZ It's OK, honey, you're in the Galaxy Health Club in New York City. *Anno domini* 2003. Calm down, nobody's going to hurt you. You're safe here. Just don't spend too much time in the whirlpool. It'll wreak havoc with your Elizabethan immune system.

OPHELIA [*Staring at Jesus' bathing suit.*] My Lord Hamlet?

ROZ Guess again. Your brother killed the bastard in a duel.

JESUS I'm Hay-zoos…the life guard.

OPHELIA Prithee, cover thyself, Sirrah.

JESUS [*Quickly covering his groin with his hands.*]
Hay-zoos Eduardo de Los Angeles Avila Morales.

ROZ Could he and Laertes just sit down over a frosty glass of mead and settle their differences like civilized human beings? No, they had to fight! Because that's what men do! Fight and go whoring after innocent girls! Don't get me started… It was one thing when Wally went after his receptionist, but a checkout girl at Duane Reade! [*Pause.*] Who the hell is Duane Reade anyway?

OPHELIA [*Singing to JESUS, suddenly flirtatious.*]

"By Gis and by Saint Charity,
Alack, and fie for shame!
Young men will do't, if they come to' it;
By cock, they are to blame.
Quoth she, before you tumbled me,
You promised me to wed."

JESUS [*Backing away from her.*]
Miss, Miss, you're mixing me up with someone else.

[OPHELIA, *who's subject to rapid mood changes, suddenly flies at* JESUS *and tries to scratch out his eyes.*]

OPHELIA *Thou dids't my noble father murder most foully! Fie on thee, Hamlet, fie! Good Polonius is dead!*

JESUS [*Trying to defend himself. In Spanish.*] Hey, watch it! You almost scratched out my eye! I didn't do anything. You're one crazy lady!

OPHELIA Murderer most foul! I smell my father's blood on thy wicked hands. Release me, I say, release me!

[*They struggle.*]

JESUS [*Letting her go.*] OK, OK...

ROZ [In a stage whisper to JESUS.] She's mad.

JESUS What did I do?

ROZ Not *angry* mad, *crazy* mad!

[ROZ *rubs her finger on her lips making crazy person sounds.* JESUS *imitates her, unsure of her meaning.*]

OPHELIA [*Rushing to the whirlpool to clean herself.*]

And now my flesh bears the marks o' your villainous hands.

ROZ Nuts! Bonkers!

[*Circling her finger next to her ear in another crazy person gesture.*]

Forget it, forget it. Don't even try to reach her. You live in different worlds.

[*Putting her hand in the whirlpool.*]

Well what do you know? The heat came back.

[*She turns on the jets and sinks down into the water.*]

Ahhhhh, this is more like it.

[*Motioning to Ophelia.*]

Come on in and join me.

[OPHELIA *tentatively gets back into the pool.* ROZ *smiles at her and rests her arms on the edge.* OPHELIA *rests her arms on the edge.* ROZ *does head rolls.* OPHELIA *does head rolls. Then she starts singing again, tossing flowers into the water.*]

OPHELIA "He is dead and gone, lady
He is dead and gone;
At his head a grass-green turf,
At his heels a stone."

JESUS [*Rushing over to the whirlpool.*]
Miss, Miss, it's against the rules to throw flowers in the pool.
You'll jam the filters.

[OPHELIA *darts up to the rim of the pool and throws in more flowers.*]

JESUS [*Grabbing her around the waist.*]

Miss, please!

[*He places her back down on the floor. Feeling his arms around her, she guides him into a brief courtly dance.*]

OPHELIA [*Suddenly pulling away.*]

Lord Hamlet, thou art much changed!

JESUS My name is Hay-zoos… Hay-zoos Avila Santa Domingo
Morales. I'm the lifeguard here. I save the drowning. Whether
they walk on land, swim the seas, or fly above. [*A pause, then he
bows and does a poignant bird call.*]

OPHELIA Thou know'st the song o' the meadow lark!

[JESUS *sings like a tortoise.*]

OPHELIA The ancient tortoise!

[JESUS *sings like a lizard.*]

OPHELIA The lowly lizard!

[JESUS *sings like a porpoise.*]

OPHELIA [*Clapping her hands with delight.*]

And e'en the paddle-billed porpoise.

[*She joins him and they sing a poignant duet together.*]

JESUS I know these songs because I was born in Costa Rica. My father was a fisherman. He caught more fish than anyone in our village. And do you know why? Because he couldn't speak like other men. He was born without a tongue. So he sharpened his ears and learned how to listen. He could hear the rain before it fell, the birds gossiping in distant jungles and the fish murmuring on the ocean floor. When he set sail in the morning, the gulls would lead him to his catch. The moment he dropped anchor, he dove into the water and swam with the very fish he was trying to lure into his nets. They told him their stories— about their ancestors who walked on land and their great cities that mysteriously sank into the sea. When I turned 12, he let me swim with him and taught me how to listen as well. Soon I was swimming great distances because the fish would guide me— showing me the safest routes and warning me of approaching storms. They'd sing to me when I got weary and spin tales about the ancient gods that once ruled the earth. Everyone thinks I swim for the glory of the miles I cover, but I do it because I long to be with the creatures of the deep. They entertain me, teach me and finally make me a better man.

OPHELIA [*With sudden gravity.*] Dost thou believe, my lord?

JESUS Believe what?

OPHELIA In a heart that's pure?

ROZ [*Under her breath.*] Lotsa luck!

OPHELIA I did possess one once, but then lost it.

JESUS Where did you lose it?

OPHELIA If I knew, t'would not be lost, my lord. And you?

JESUS What about me?

OPHELIA Where is thy heart?

JESUS [*After a brief pause.*] In your hands.

[ROZ *mimes playing a violin.*]

JESUS All I've ever cared about was swimming, but now that I've met you...I...I...

OPHELA [*Excited.*] *Thou swim'st?*

JESUS Great distances. Next month I attempt the English Channel.

OPHELIA The *English*, Channel, my lord? In faith, I've crossed it oft!

JESUS Thou swim'st too? I knew it! I knew it!

OPHELIA [*Momentarily lucid.*] No, my lord, I crossed it in a ship. In my youth our family summered oft in England. We traveled by coach to Calais and thence set sail for Dover. Verily, they were the happiest o' times...Laertes and I wouldst clamber to the top o' the crow's nest and there peruse the changing horizon. At eventide, our father, good Polonius joined us in our swaying perch. He knew each constellation's place and wouldst point them out to us.

[*As Polonius.*] "There's Orion's Belt, mark it well...! And there, wretched Callista, the great bear who weeps for her son, she unwittingly slayed with her own hand."

Laertes and I hung on his every word, his voice sinking and rising wi' the swells that bore us o'er the waves. Verily, he conversed wi' the wind itself, waving his arms as if swapping tales wi' a dear old friend. Twas he, my star-gazing father, who unfurled the twin maps that bind the earth—the constellations that wink above and the oceans that slumber below. Twas those very maps that guided me 'neath the waters o' the earth til I popped of a sudden into this...bubbling pool.

[*She returns to the pool and gazes into its depths.*]

JESUS Marry me!

OPHELIA My lord?

JESUS You're my other half! The bride I've been waiting for.

[*He gently kisses her.*]

OPHELIA [*Moving away from him.*] My lord!

JESUS My father told me I'd find you one day.

OPHELIA In faith, I didst love thee once.

JESUS Together we'll swim the waters of the earth!

OPHELIA But then thou came'st to me in my closet, ..."like sweet bells jangled, out of tune and harsh..."

JESUS "Sweet bells jangled?"

OPHELIA "That unmatcht form and feature of blown youth Blasted with ecstasy..."

JESUS Yes, ecstasy! Ecstasy!

OPHELIA [*Pulling away.*]

"O woe is me, t'have seen what I have seen, see what I see."

JESUS I don't care where I swim anymore—the Indian Ocean or the Dead Sea... I just want to be at your side. Hand in hand. Seeing together... listening together... moving through the water together...

[*Moving in to kiss her again.*]

ROZ [*Feigning a sudden asthma attack.*]

HELP...HELP...JESUS, I CAN'T BREATHE! I NEED MY INHALER! MY INHALER...

JESUS [*Rushing over to her.*]

Easy, easy, don't panic...

ROZ [*Gasping for air.*] HURRY! MY INHALER... IT'S IN MY LOCKER... NUMBER 55...

[*Taking the keys off from around her wrist and throwing them at him.*]

HERE ARE THE KEYS. QUICKLY, QUICKLY... I CAN'T BREATHE... I can't breathe...

[*She puts on quite a show, clutching her chest and making a variety of unearthly noises.*]

JESUS [*Exiting as fast as he can.*] Locker 55?

ROZ Hurry...Hurry...

OPHELIA [*Bending over her.*] My lady?

ROZ [*Recovering.*] It's alright... I just wanted to get rid of him. "Too much of water hast thou poor Ophelia." You need a rest! Not some hot-blooded marathon swimmer to drag you all over the map. And who's to say he wouldn't ditch you for some hot little mermaid sunning herself off a spit of sand on St. Tropez. You'd be better off on dry land... With Duane Reade! [Pause.] *Him* again! Why does his name keep coming up? Because his drug stores are on every goddamned street corner. Talk about overkill...! *Men!* Take my advice and forget the lot of them!

[*Grabbing her arm and speaking with great authority as Hamlet.*]

"Get thee to a nunnery."

OPHELIA Why are those words so familiar? Verily, Hamlet spake them to me, 'nary a moment ago!

ROZ I didn't get a chronic asthma condition teaching Shakespeare in the public school system for nothing!

[*Leading* OPHELIA *back into the whirlpool.*]

"Why wouldst thou be a breeder of sinners? I am myself indifferent honest: but yet I could accuse me of such things that it were better my mother had not borne me... I am very proud, revengful, ambitious; with more offences at my beck than I have thoughts to put them in, imagination to give them shape, or time to act them in. What should such fellows as I do crawling between earth and heaven? We are arrant knaves, all; believe none of us. Go thy ways to a nunnery... If thou dost marry, I'll give thee this plague for thy dowry, —be thou as chaste as ice, as pure as snow, thou shalt not escape calumny. Get thee to a nunnery, go: farewell..."

[*As herself again, pushing* OPHELIA *under water.*]

I'm doing this for your own good, believe me!

OPHELIA [*Disappearing.*]
"I thank you for your good counsel. Come, my coach! —Good night ladies; good night sweet ladies: good night, good night."

[*And she's gone.*]

ROZ Now...how do you drain this damned thing? There must be a plug somewhere on the bottom... Ah here it is!

[*She dramatically pulls it out.*]

[*There's a terrific sound of water slurping down the drain. ROZ struggles not to be sucked down as well.*]

JESUS [*From offstage.*]

I'VE GOT IT! I'VE GOT YOUR INHALER! YOU MUST HAVE GIVEN ME YOUR HOUSE KEYS BY MISTAKE.

[*Roz quickly sneaks out of the room.*]

JESUS I COULDN'T OPEN THE LOCK AND HAD TO BREAK DOWN THE DOOR!

[*Running in.*]

Hey, where did everybody go?

[*Rushing into the whirlpool.*]

Ophelia... Ophelia... Where are you? What happened to all the water?

[*Breaking down, speaking in Spanish as the swooning Allegro molto from Handel's Suite No. 1 starts to play.*]

Ofelia, Ofelia, regressa! Te amo. Ibamos a nadar las aguas del mundo, mi media naranja, mi novia acuatica, mi delfin del fondo, mi estrellita del mar. Con tus manos siento, con tu boca canto, y con tus pulmones respiro. Ofelia, Ofelia, Salvame! Que me ahogo!

[*The lights slowly fade on his heartbroken face.*]

[*As the curtain slowly falls.*]

[*English translation.*] Ophelia, Ophelia, come back! I love you! We were going to swim the oceans together...You're my other half...my shining starfish, my plunging porpoise, my watery bride...I feel through your hands, sing through your voice and breathe through your lungs. Ophelia, Ophelia, save me...I'm drowning...

• • •

Ten-Dollar Drinks

Joe Pintauro

Joe Pintauro

Joe Pintauro's three one-act plays about Italian American life in New York City, *Cacciatore*, earned his first major theatre reviews. *Snow Orchid*, his first full-length play, became a selection of the Eugene O'Neill Conference and was later staged with Olympia Dukakis, Peter Boyle and Robert Lupone at New York's Circle Rep. A revival in London starred Jude Law and Paola di Ognisotti. His short plays *American Divine* and *Moving Targets* have been compared to James Joyce's *The Dubliners*. Pintauro's full-length plays include *Beside Herself*, staged with William Hurt, Lois Smith, Calista Flockhart and Melissa Joan Hart, and *Raft of The Medusa*. *Men's Lives*, an adaptation of Peter Matthiessen's non-fiction book, was the inaugural production of the Bay Street Theatre in Sag Harbor, New York. *The Dead Boy*, about faith and trauma, workshopped at London's Royal Court under Stephen Daldry and again there with Ian McKellen. Pintauro directed *The Dead Boy* in Dutch in the Netherlands as *Dode Jongen*, with Anton Lutz and most recently with Roy Scheider and Mercedes Ruehl, again in workshop in Key West. His collection of 40 short plays, *Metropolitan Operas* (Dramatists Play Service, New York), are produced in various languages worldwide including at the Comedia del Arte in Venetia under Carla Poli.

The trilogy *By The Sea, By The Sea, By The Beautiful Sea*, a collaboration with Terrence McNally and Lanford Wilson, was produced by The Bay Street Theatre and The Manhattan Theatre Club. *Heaven And Earth*, about American farm life, also a Bay Street production, was directed by Jack Hofsiss. Pintauro has recently completed *Beautiful Dreamer*, a Civil War screenplay about the only woman to ever receive the Congressional Medal of Honor, and is working on two new full-length plays with The Pacific Theatre Company, in Los Angeles, *Karma Boomerang* and *Dance Nite On The River Queen*.

The Dead Boy was a selection of the Eugene O'Neill Playwrights Conference. His novel *State of Grace* was published by Times Books. His novel *Cold Hands* (Simon and Schuster) was widely reviewed and singled out by *The New York Times* as one of the best novels of the year. He was recently awarded the Margaret Hill inaugural chair in theatre at Saint Mary's College, Notre Dame, and was named a recipient of the 2005 John Steinbeck award for literature.

characters

STAR Thirty or over.

BETE Thirty or over.

setting

A drinks table at the Russian Tea Room.

. . .

[STAR *is extremely well dressed,* BETE, *less so.*]

STAR I mean *everyone* was there. Everyone.

BETE The only stars I give a damn about are the ones on my kid's report card.

STAR How is he...uh...

BETE You forgot his name.

STAR Jesse.

BETE You forgot before you remembered. Just the way you saw me that night at Allison's, and lousy actress that you are you screwed up pretending not to see me.

STAR I saw you at Allison's.

BETE You are the worst.

STAR I was surrounded by twenty sycophantic moving mouths.

BETE Congratulations! Congratulations! But meantime we waited on your leash for you to say hi...

STAR I had another party to go to.

BETE We figured as much my dear, but we refused to suffer the ignominy of you leaving first and waving us pathetic *"Dear, what can I do?"*

STAR Talk about your son. That calms you.

BETE He got into Trinity.

STAR I presume that's good news.

BETE In my world it is.

STAR Well, that's nice.

BETE Till my money runs out. And don't you interpret that as I got you here to ask for a handout.

STAR Thanks. Here's to Jesse.

BETE That I'll drink to.

STAR Why'd you pick a place where the drinks are ten bucks?

BETE Me, invite a star to a no-class joint?

STAR I'll pick up the check if you let me.

BETE You bet your sweet ass I'll let you.

STAR What about all that voice-over work?

BETE New producer, new voice. Yesterday I got a call for a denture spot.

STAR You didn't.

BETE Old people are getting younger every day, honey.

STAR In L.A. they said you're up for that Pinter thing.

BETE Yeah.

STAR Tired?

BETE Just pissed. At my husband for being a drunk, my parents for dying, the dying was bad enough but leaving me shit...

STAR Uh... What the hell time is it?

BETE Now tell me you've got to go.

STAR No, go on...your husband?

BETE I went and fell in love with an actor who hates himself, what else is new, except this one's a drunk so I go ahead and have his kid.

STAR You're talkin' about your son now.

BETE A terrific kid, knock wood.

STAR Does he see his dad?

BETE From a cab a couple weeks ago we saw him in rotted jogging shoes with glassy eyes, walking his dog.

STAR I thought he got himself a soap.

BETE He's on the "World" thing or "The Bold and the Broken."

STAR Then he should help with Jesse.

BETE He sends some money.

[STAR *stares as to ask, "Then why kvetch?"*]

STAR I hate to say this, but I got a damn P.R. meeting. So...what is it? I showed up. So?

BETE Okay. I'm not jealous of you.

STAR That's it?

BETE Before we drift apart, as we obviously will, and you decide you don't know me at all anymore, I want in the record that I'll never envy you no matter what you accumulate, acquire...

STAR You've got too much on the ball to envy anybody.

BETE True.

STAR Too bad the rest of the world hasn't acknowledged this.

BETE That's okay...

[*The insult catches up to her.*]

Let's keep it between you and me shall we?

[*Now letting it show.*]

I'm not ashamed to look you in the eye and show you the hurt I feel.

STAR Hurt for yourself or me?

BETE Hurt that you walk around this town like you never knew a lot of your old friends.

STAR Oh, Jesus.

BETE Oh, Jesus, huh?

STAR I win that cursed thing and suddenly I need four telephones and still I have to hire someone around the apartment to screen my callers. I hear from high-school friends, relatives I never met. I'm a freak. I'm worn out...

BETE We acted in the same company for ten years. We ate more dinners, spent more rotten hours together. I paid for more coffees. We slept together more nights...

STAR You're not going around claiming that.

BETE You dog. I meant I had to put you to sleep, you drunk, on my couch a half dozen times. I'm not claiming to be your sister or some high-school jerk. You always were using everyone, everything. And it worked. What are you complaining about? So here's to your fucking obese ego, your obscene Oscar and your fame.

[*Star pushes her drink.*]

STAR You know what fame is? Multiply all the people you don't wanna know by two hundred million. That's fame. Fame...is the drink that comes to your table from that dark corner of the restaurant and it could be from either a deranged stalker or your future lover. Either way if you don't drink the shit they'll hate you till they die. There is nothing spiritual about fame. Fame is prostitution without body contact. I know only one person who believed she was a true goddess. She refused to go to the bathroom because it would destroy her status and she wound up exploding in a Los Angeles emergency room. That's fame, Honey.

BETE Well, it didn't look that way at the Academy Awards.

STAR [*With fear of the jealousy and the punishment.*] Did you watch?

BETE You looked great. You said exactly the right thing. I was proud.

STAR But did you watch?

BETE Well, of course I watched.

STAR Katie and Bill didn't watch. It's amazing how many didn't bother.

BETE I can't believe Katie didn't watch it.

STAR They had a gallery opening.

BETE She saw it on the news, didn't she?

STAR They saw nothing.

BETE   She didn't see the *paper?*

STAR   She said it wasn't delivered that day.

BETE   That bitch.

STAR   Well, nobody expected I'd get it, least of all me.

BETE   *I* didn't expect you to *get* it. You were up there with ancient deities, for heaven's sake.

STAR   Cut the bullshit.

BETE   Why? It's never for us to judge this stuff. So maybe you didn't deserve it…

STAR   I didn't say I didn't deserve it. Oh you…

BETE   I just hate you for going off into the sunset like some Wagnerian myth.

STAR   You're a better actress than I.

BETE   Just not as lucky as you. Is that the message?

STAR   You know you never were my best friend, for cryin' out loud.

BETE   But so unknown I deserved to be snubbed? You want me to buy that you don't know me at all? Ask me, I'll pretend we never met. Oh, you should be punished. God…

STAR   Oh, c'mon. Hey.

BETE   It's like watching a ship sailing away forever.

STAR   For me it's like being *on* the ship.

BETE   I never had so close a friend win one of those horrid things.

STAR   Why don't you stop wasting time and tell me to my face that you're jealous of me.

BETE What? I would despise myself if I felt one ounce...of...of jealousy of you of all people. I'm a damned good actress, better than most of the clowns out there.

STAR Including me.

BETE Yes, and you said it yourself. And I'd hate myself if I stooped to...to...jealousy...or...

STAR Then you hate yourself.

BETE You sonofabitch. I don't hate myself for having my son, for...for...

STAR Your son has nothing to do with this.

BETE I couldn't drag my ass around La-La Land with that kid.

STAR I didn't make it in L.A. I made it here on the same stage, in the same company as you.

BETE [*Ping pong.*] I waited on tables. You've been subsidized since you were born.

STAR I worked my ass off.

BETE You're still not good enough.

STAR So why don't you throw your drink in my face? You've been dying to since you walked in here.

BETE Ach...throw my *drink*?

STAR Your hand's been shaking. You can hardly hold it back. Go ahead. Someone may take a picture. You'll get in the papers. People will gossip about it. You'll be welded to me for life. Maybe it'll get you a part in something.

BETE   You weirdo.

STAR   Oh, cut the shit. You're just as fucking hard-hearted an entrepreneur as I am. For a month you've been trying to provoke this argument. I'm here. I showed up. So go prove to the world you're intimate with a star...

BETE   You know what a star is? You piece of shit? A star is one of those gorgeous goddamn glittering things in the heavens that mankind has been staring at for millions of years. It's a fucking *sun*, a giant, burning, eternal glory that gives more life than all our little fat heads put together cannot imagine. The kind of star you are is the paper kind, with glue on the back, the kind you buy by the hundreds in a little box for a buck.

STAR   Cut the monologue and throw the fuckin' drink in my face.

[BETE *stands in horror.*]

BETE   I'm getting out of here, you crazy sonofabitch.

STAR   Sure, because I'm wise to you. You aren't jealous, merely jealous. You're the same predatory opportunist you always were. You played your last card to get me here and you won. I'm bending to you, paying my dues so you can cut yourself in for your share of the pie. Well, take your share. Throw the goddamn drink. Throw the glass.

[BETE *lifts her drink and flings it into* STAR'*s face. The two continue to look at one another.* BETE *starts to leave.*]

Come back. Sit. Sit down.

[BETE *sits slowly, totally emptied of feeling.* STAR *grabs her hand and puts it to her cheek. She kisses* BETE'*s hand gratefully, as* BETE *looks on, amazed and stunned.*]

• • •